Avoiding Untimely Death

"This powerful and timely book is more than an exposition—it is a spiritual wake-up call. With deep scriptural insight and prophetic clarity, the author addresses the pressing issue of untimely death and reveals how believers can walk in spiritual authority to fulfill their God-ordained destiny. Unazi Ogah makes it clear: death is not always on God's terms. Sin, disobedience, spiritual ignorance, and lack of warfare can open the door to premature departure. But through faith, obedience, and intimacy with God, we can walk in preservation and purpose. Each chapter is filled with biblical truths, practical counsel, and anointing to ignite deeper pursuit of God."

—FELIX BAMIRIN,
Pastor, Graceway Church, Austin, Texas

"In *Avoiding Untimely Death*, Unazi offers a powerful, truth-filled guide to living a long and purposeful life. Just as a doctor prescribes a diet for health, this book prescribes godly habits and attitudes for spiritual and physical longevity. Unazi reminds us that sin and disobedience bring death, but obedience to God's word brings life. Clear, practical, and deeply rooted in Scripture, this book is a must-read for all seeking divine direction for lasting life."

—CHARLES SAWADOGO,
Lead Pastor, New Creation Church, Austin, Texas

"In *Avoiding Untimely Death*, Unazi Ogah has given us an outstanding and timely gift. Ogah focuses us on Gods plan for us—that we fulfill our days by bearing fruit for His glory (John 15:8). Combining biblical promises and examples of the Holy Spirit at work, this book will call many back to God, will ignite fresh devotion to Jesus, and will result in us fulfilling our days in Him. This book is for you!"

—GRAHAM ALLEN,
Church Pastor, Brownwood, TX

"*Avoiding Untimely Death* is a must-read for those living in 2025! Death has plagued the country through sickness, violence, and various accidents. In this book, author Unazi Ogah gives the reader key insights into ways the reader can draw close to the Lord, take responsibility, and stifle the enemy's plan to kill, steal, and destroy our lives. Ogah lists the enemy's traps and the mistakes that lead believers to untimely death."

—JACOB PEARSON,
Graduate Student, Global Awakening Theological Seminary

"In this title, Unazi has shared a divine message on how to fulfill one's given mandate, divine assignment, and live a life well pleasing to God. A great reminder of God's heart and desire for humanity. May the message of this book spur you to action as you seek to live for Him and do His will."

—STEPHEN T. ADEGBITE,
Katy, Texas

Avoiding Untimely Death

Discover How You Can Live and Fulfill Your Days

UNAZI OGAH

RESOURCE *Publications* • Eugene, Oregon

AVOIDING UNTIMELY DEATH
Discover How You Can Live and Fulfill Your Days

Resource Publications
An Imprint of Wipf and Stock Publishers
199 W. 8th Ave., Suite 3
Eugene, OR 97401

www.wipfandstock.com

PAPERBACK ISBN: 979-8-3852-4800-1
HARDCOVER ISBN: 979-8-3852-4801-8
EBOOK ISBN: 979-8-3852-4802-5

06/04/25

Contents

Preface

Several years ago, while still a teenager and at the beginning of my walk with Christ, I had a remarkable prophetic dream that will form the basis of this book. In that dream, I witnessed several people dying: women and children, old and young. I grieved and sad and was weeping profusely in the dream, and I could recall asking God, "Why is all this happening?" "Why are people dying everywhere?" and the voice of God spoke from heaven and said to me, "Yes, people are dying, but you will not die until you accomplish the plan I have for you." This revelation completely changed my perspective of death. It gave me an unshakable faith in the power of God to keep me alive until I do precisely all He has called me to do.

Based on my understanding of this prophetic dream, I am writing this book so that the reader can understand death from God's perspective and learn how to stay alive until they accomplish God's will.

This book is for anyone worried about dying unfulfilled—dying while they still have more to give to the world, dying before they have emptied themselves of all the wisdom and knowledge that God has placed within them. Since death affects everyone, this book is for everyone, not just believers in Jesus Christ.

This book will not only explain untimely death and how God sees it but also provide you with the tools to avoid dying before you fulfill your God-appointed days on earth (Psalm 139:16). It will also delve into the genesis of death, various sources of untimely death, and what you should do to stay alive until you have lived your life to the fullest. You will feel reassured and comforted by the end, with a newfound understanding of death and a path to overcome your fear.

I want to thank my God for allowing me to write this book. I thank Him for the wisdom, revelational knowledge, and for counting me worthy to share His truth with my generation. To Him be glory forever and ever. Amen

I want to thank my beloved wife, Rebecca Ogah, for all her support and encouragement to continue doing what God has called me to do and for being a faithful wife to me and a lovely mother to our three beautiful children. May my God continue to bless her and keep her.

I would also like to express my heartfelt thanks to my reviewers—Stephen Adegbite, Pastor Graham Allen, Jacob Pearson, Pastor Felix Bamirin, and Pastor Charles Sawadogo—for their time and effort in reviewing this book. Your thoughtful feedback significantly contributed to enhancing its quality. May the Lord bless you richly. Thank you.

Finally, please read and meditate on this book. Don't doubt the knowledge of God revealed in it; it will give you complete confidence in God's power, eliminate the fear of death for good, and set you on a path toward fulfilling your God-given mission on earth. Praise God!

Introduction

When we talk about dying an untimely death, we are referring to departing this world without fulfilling the divine plan God has for you. This untimely death is not what people typically consider untimely; it is what God, in His infinite wisdom, deems untimely. God said,

> "My ways are not your ways, neither are My thoughts your thoughts" (Isaiah 55:8 NKJV).

This verse reminds us that our understanding of time and fulfillment differs from God's. Someone may die young in the eyes of men, but in the eyes of God, that person may have lived a fulfilled life and completed the number of days ordained by God. This is echoed in Psalm 139:16, which says,

> "Your eyes saw my unformed body; all the days ordained for me were written in your book before one of them came to be."

For example, Jesus Christ was crucified at the age of 33, which, by human standards, is a very young age to leave this world. However, He fulfilled His days and glorified God on earth. He knew the hour of His death and even the manner of His death. Unlike many who live long but never accomplish God's will, Jesus' mission was complete, proving that fulfillment is not measured by years but in accomplishing God's purpose. Therefore, I define untimely death as dying without fulfilling the number of days ordained by God for you on earth.

Every believer must grasp that God has already determined the number of days you will live on earth, even before you were conceived in your mother's womb. This 'number of days' is not just a numerical value but a divine plan for your life that includes fulfilling God's purpose for you, your impact on others, and the lessons you will learn. Psalm 90:12 wisely states,

> "So teach us to number our days, that we may gain a heart of wisdom" (Psalm 90:12 NKJV).

Acknowledging that your days are numbered is a mark of great wisdom. Those who live reckless lives often fail to comprehend this truth, leading them to fall into foolish ways and what the Bible calls the 'ways of death' (Proverbs 14:12 NKJV). These 'ways of death' are not just physical destruction but include a life lived outside of God's direction—walking in rebellion, pursuing self-centered ambitions, and ignoring divine counsel. The 'ways of death' refer to a life lived without God's guidance, a life that ultimately leads to spiritual death and separation from God. This is not just physical death but a state of being disconnected from God's purpose and plan for your life. That is the consequence of not living according to God's plan.

Untimely death, as we understand it, means departing before your God-ordained time on earth or before living out God's plan for your life. There are many instances in Scripture where people departed before fulfilling God's plan for their lives—Onan (Genesis 38:9-10), Rachel (Genesis 35:19), the generation of Israelites who perished in the wilderness (Numbers 14:29-35), King Saul (1 Samuel 31:4-6; cf. 1 Samuel 13:13-14), Judas Iscariot (Matthew 27:5; Acts 1:18-20), and others. Subsequent chapters will delve into these examples in greater detail.

The most fulfilling way to depart from this world is when God calls you home after fully embracing and living out His plan for your life. This is the reason for your existence. You did not enter this world by your own choice; you did not select your parents, your country, or the time of your birth (Psalm 139:16). The Creator meticulously planned every aspect of your life even before you were conceived. Your life is not an accident, and every moment is divinely orchestrated. Therefore, living your life as God intended and dying the death that God ordained for you is the epitome of a successful life and a life well-lived in the eyes of God. To fulfill your days and depart this world at God's appointed time, having walked in His will, is the truest definition of a life well-lived. Praise God!

Don't Die Before Your Time

To everything, there is a season, a time to be born, and a time to die. (Ecclesiastics 3:1–8 NKJV)

Your Divine Purpose

God meticulously planned your life before your conception. You are not a product of chance but a deliberate creation of God's perfect plan. Even amid human error, God's divine plan prevails, using even our mistakes to fulfill His purpose.

> *"Before I formed you in the womb I knew you; Before you were born I sanctified you; I ordained you a prophet to the nations"* (Jeremiah 1:5 NKJV)

As 2 Timothy 1:9 states,

> *"who has saved us and called us with a holy calling, not according to our works, but according to His own purpose and grace which was given to us in Christ Jesus before time began."*

God knew you before you were born and ordained you for a specific purpose in Christ. Some will say that this scripture refers to the prophet Jeremiah, but it does not distinguish him from any man born into the world.

This scripture reveals a profound truth: Your existence predates your birth. God knew you even before you were formed in the womb, a testament to your eternal significance in His eyes.

"For You formed my inward parts; You covered me in my mother's womb. I will praise You, for I am fearfully and wonderfully made; Marvelous are Your works, And my soul knows very well. My frame was not hidden from You, When I was made in secret, And skillfully wrought in the lowest parts of the earth. Your eyes saw my substance, being yet unformed. And in Your book, they all were written, The days fashioned for me, When as yet there were none of them." (Psalm 139:13–16 NKJV)

This scripture shows that God formed you in your mother's womb. God carefully made all the intricate parts of your body. He knows you even more than you know yourself.

He also ordained the number of days you are to spend on earth. God decided your days on earth even before you were born.

Understanding God's Sovereignty and Our Responsibility

The Psalmist says My times are in your hand, O God.

"My times are in Your hand; Deliver me from the hand of my enemies, And from those who persecute me" (Psalm 31:15 NKJV).

David said in Psalm 31:15, "My times are in your hands." So, the times of your life are in God's hands. But someone may ask, if they are in God's hands, why can you die before your time? That is an excellent question to ask. However, if you see the scripture in Psalm 31:15, you can see that after David said that his times are in God's hands, he immediately prayed to God to deliver him from all his enemies and those who persecuted him. So we see that even though he knew his life was in God's hands, he understood that there was a possibility that he could lose his life if God didn't intervene.

So, just because God planned and ordained something for your life doesn't mean it will happen as God intended. Jesus said we should pray for God's will to be done on earth as it is in heaven (Matt. 6:10). Most of the happenings on earth are not God's will (Matt. 6:10): death, hunger, sickness, wars, and many more. All these unfortunate events are not the will of God for humanity. They are consequences of rebellion, misalignment, and humanity's rejection of God (1 John 5:19).

The Role of Prayer and Alignment in Fulfilling God's Plan

It is not enough to simply know God's plan for your life. You have the power to enforce that plan through the transformative act of prayer and alignment with God's will.

God has already prophesied everything about your life, even before you were conceived. Remember, God is good, and every good thing comes from Him. This knowledge should fill you with hope and optimism.

> *"For I know the thoughts that I think toward you, says the Lord, thoughts of peace and not of evil, to give you a future and a hope"* (Jeremiah 29:11 NKJV).

God has a very, very good plan for your life. Any evil you experience or heartbreak doesn't come from God. We know that the evil that befalls humanity does not come from God.

> *"Every good gift and every perfect gift is from above, and comes down from the Father of lights, with whom there is no variation or shadow of turning"* (James 1:17 NKJV).

Every good and every perfect gift comes from God. Therefore, we can say that anything that is not good and perfect is not from God.

Understanding the Source of Adversity in Our Lives

God plans to bring you to an expected end, and sometimes, He may turn adversity around and make it work for your ultimate good. However, that does not mean that the adversity came from God. Even if it ends well for you, it doesn't mean the adversity came from God. God can give you deliverance from your enemies, but that doesn't mean God sent those enemies after your life (Genesis 50:20).

The scripture says God cannot be tempted with evil; neither does He tempt any man with evil.

> "Let no one say when he is tempted, 'God tempts me'; for
> God cannot be tempted by evil, nor does He tempt anyone"
> (James 1:13 NKJV).

God will not bring evil into your life to prove a point. Many of the evils you face in life are either self-inflicted or coming from the enemies of your soul.

Discerning the Seasons of Your Life

Not only will God not bring evil your way, but He will also let you know the season of your life if you are close to Him so that nothing will surprise you.

For example, everything has a season (Eccl 3:1). Knowing the season of your life is a sign that you are in close contact with God (1 Chronicles 12:32).

It is good to know the seasons of your life and their times. When the time comes for a particular season, and you are not experiencing it, you can wage war in the spirit to bring that season into existence (1 Chronicles 12:32).

The Connection Between Prophecy and Spiritual Warfare

This brings us to an important point: God's prophecies and other things written about your life will require your cooperation to come to pass. If you are unaware of these things, you cannot engage in the necessary spiritual warfare to bring them to pass. Understanding this concept should prepare you for the challenges of life.

> *"This charge I commit to you, son Timothy, according to the prophecies previously made concerning you, that by them you may wage the good warfare"* (1 Timothy 1:18 NKJV)

Here, Paul is telling Timothy to fight the war in the spirit so that God's promises concerning him will come to pass (Hebrews 10:7).

Lack of awareness and lack of accurate spiritual warfare are the reasons many people experience many things that God did not plan for their lives.

Understanding Untimely Death in God's Plan

For example, people die before their God-ordained time. Someone may say, how would you know if a person dies before the time ordained by God? People who died unprepared for their death and all those who died without doing the things they set out to accomplish in life, if at the time of death, they wish they had more time, then they are dying before their God-ordained time. God will never allow any of His servants to die before their time. In the scriptures, even prophets of God whose lives were cut short, God allowed them to die because, at the time of death, they had already fulfilled the plan of God for their lives.

Not every prophet or believer is destined to live for a very long time. If they are messengers of God, they don't need to preach to many people before their assignment is over. God may raise a prophet to preach just one message before they are killed or martyred for their testimony.

"Then the Spirit of God came upon Zechariah the son of Jehoiada the priest, who stood above the people, and said to them, 'Thus says God: "Why do you transgress the commandments of the Lord, so that you cannot prosper? Because you have forsaken the Lord, He also has forsaken you."' So they conspired against him, and at the command of the king they stoned him with stones in the court of the house of the Lord." (2 Chronicles 24:20–21 NKJV)

In this scripture, we see that Zechariah, the priest who was also a prophet, was killed after he gave them the message from God. That was the only recorded time the Spirit of God came upon him, and he gave only that message before the people killed him. Someone may say he died untimely and without fulfillment. Still, in God's eyes, he died fulfilling God's purpose, and his death was a testimony against the evil being perpetuated by the people of Israel at that time. We have several instances like this in the Bible where a servant of God was murdered for their testimony, beginning with Abel, whom Cain killed (Genesis 4:8). It may seem as though these people died untimely, but looking at this from God's perspective, this was not the case. If you are a servant of God, you cannot die no matter what befalls you, except God allows that physical death to happen. For God to allow it to happen, it will mean that you have already accomplished God's plan for your life.

Biblical Examples of God's Protection and Timing

We have biblical precedents for this; we saw how God preserved Joseph's life until he accomplished God's plan (Genesis 50:20, 45:7). We saw how God preserved Moses, right from when he was born as a child when he could have easily been killed according to the decree made by the king pharaoh to have all boy children killed; God preserved his life even when he fled pharaoh for his life, God preserved him until about age eighty, when He appeared in the burning bush and revealed His plan for Israel (Exodus 3:1–10; Acts 7:30). He then led the nation for roughly forty more years, dying at the ripe age of 120 (Exodus 7:7; Deuteronomy 34:7). We saw how God preserved the life of David and kept him alive until he became king of Israel. We saw how God kept prophet Jeremiah alive despite multiple attempts on his life until he had prophesied all the prophecies that God wanted him to give to the children of Israel. We saw how God protected Jesus Christ from the Pharisees until the hour of his death, when Judas betrayed him into their hand. What about Peter, Paul, and John the Beloved Apostle? God kept every one of them alive by His supernatural power until the appointed time of their departure. God is sovereign because nothing in heaven, on earth, or underneath the earth happens without His knowledge.

*"Whatever the Lord pleases He does, In heaven and earth,
In the seas and all deep places"* (Psalm 135:6 NKJV)

Therefore, we can say when a servant of God is killed or martyred, and God allowed it to happen, then their death, no matter how horrible or the circumstance that brought their death, we can still say it pleases God for it to be so. This is hard to understand from the natural man's perspective. But spiritually speaking, that is what is happening.

Also, the scripture says in Psalm 116:15,

"Precious in the sight of the Lord Is the death of His saints"

The Divine Protection Over God's People

So God is pleased to welcome His saint home any day, any time. What does this tell you? It implies that no one connected to God can leave this earth without God's approval. If you are in tune with heaven, God will keep you alive until you accomplish His plan for your life.

The scripture says,

"Surely the eyes of the LORD are on those who fear Him, those who hope in His mercy to deliver their souls from death and to keep them alive in the midst of famine."
(Psalm 33:18 NKJV)

The advantage of having a robust relationship with God cannot be overemphasized when it comes to avoiding untimely death. Being close to God ensures that you understand the seasons and times of your life. God will reveal to you what to do when the seasons are withheld or when the wrong season comes. Understanding the seasons and times of your life allows you to engage in effective spiritual warfare that will enforce God's will for your life.

For example, if you search the scriptures, you will find out that many of God's prophets and apostles became aware of their death season. They may not have known the exact time, hour, or manner of death they would go through, but when they were to face death, their spirit became aware of it even before it happened. Many of them were allowed to say goodbye or say their last words. When you have God, you can't die unfulfilled; you will die fulfilled no matter what time or how it happens. With God, you never lose, whether in life or death. You will always win. Hallelujah!

God's word guaranteed that if your death did not bring any gain to you or God, it wouldn't happen (Psalm 116:15). The Lord shall preserve you from all evil, including the evil of untimely death (Psalm 121:7). Be rest assured about this and be confident in this promise of God. I know death is happening everywhere around you, and it doesn't seem realistic to expect that you can understand your season of death, and it doesn't seem realistic to have faith that you can't die unexpectedly.

The scripture says,

> "Because you have made the Lord, who is my refuge, Even the Most High, your dwelling place. No evil shall befall you, Nor shall any plague come near your dwelling;" (Psalm 91:9–10 NKJV)

Psalm 121:7 says,

> "The Lord shall preserve your soul from all evil."

Death is not excluded among this evil; there is an evil death and a death that is not (Numbers 23:10). God will deliver you from the death that will bring evil to you or those close to you. Praise the LORD! That is the promise of God. Hallelujah! It doesn't matter how many people are dying around you. The scripture says in Psalm 91:7,

> "A thousand may fall at your side, And ten thousand at your right hand, But it shall not come near you."

Don't worry; you are not dying before accomplishing God's will for your life. Amen.

Seven Key Strategies to Avoid Untimely Death

So, what should you do to avoid untimely death? In this section, I will list what you can do to prevent untimely death and discuss them in greater detail in subsequent chapters.

1. Enter the Kingdom of Light

The first thing is that you have to make sure you are in the kingdom of light. Make sure you have been translated from the kingdom of darkness into the kingdom of light through repentance and faith in Jesus Christ. (1 Peter 2:9). Those who are in the kingdom of darkness are in captivity and under the power of Satan. As captives, their lives can be cut short at any time (Proverbs 2:21–22, Proverbs 24:19–20). Satan can take their life anytime, especially to make sure they never get the opportunity again to see the light of God and save their soul. Make sure you have been saved and are now under the power of God and the kingdom of God.

2. Avoid Habits That Lead to Spiritual Bondage

The second thing is that you must avoid habits that can bring you back into spiritual bondage. Galatians 5:1 says,

> "Stand fast therefore in the liberty by which Christ has made us free, and do not be entangled again with a yoke of bondage."

9

Christ has set you free just as the scripture says in John 8:36 who the Son of Man shall set free is indeed free. Nevertheless, as stated in Galatians 5:1, there is a possibility of getting entangled back into bondage again.

People are taken into captivity through sin. Sin is what the devil uses spiritually to bring people into bondage. For instance if you start lying, and before you know it, you become a slave to lies, and you can't say anything without lying. You are in bondage. Satan came to Jesus to see if he could find something in Jesus that could make him take Him captive. In John 14:30, Jesus says, "The prince of this world comes and hath nothing in me."

"Don't be deceived, and do not be ignorant of the devil's devices"(2 Corinthians 2:11 NKJV).

Your ignorance will not save your soul. If you have something that belongs to the devil in your life, he will legally lay claim on you. But thanks be to God, God has made Christ Jesus the sacrifice for your sins, so when you sin (although it is expected that you should not sin), quickly confess the sin, and God will wash away that sin from you, and you will be clean, and the devil won't find anything in you.

Unless your transgressions are taken away, the devil has legal grounds to enter your life and carry out his will. Your transgressions cannot be taken away unless you confess and forsake them. But when you acknowledge them, God will remove your transgressions far from you. The scripture says,

"As far as the east is from the west, So far has He removed our transgressions from us" (Psalm 103:12 NKJV).

"My little children, these things I write to you, so that you may not sin. And if anyone sins, we have an Advocate with the Father, Jesus Christ the righteous. And He is the propitiation for our sins, not only for ours but also the whole world." (1 John 2:1 NKJV)

3. Maintain the Practice of Confession and Repentance

God expects you not to sin in Christ Jesus (Ephesians 1:4), but it is not the end of the world if you do sin. Confess your sins, and God is faithful to forgive you.

> *"If we confess our sins, He is faithful and just to forgive us our sins and to cleanse us from all unrighteousness."* (1 John 1:9 NKJV)

It says if we confess our sins and turn away from them, He is faithful to forgive us and to cleanse us from all unrighteousness. It is not enough to confess; the scripture clearly says you should turn away from sin. If you confess and keep sinning the same sin without turning away from it, then you are taking the blood of Jesus Christ for granted and as an uncommon thing. This is something we are warned not to do. The scriptures say,

> *"Of how much worse punishment, do you suppose, will he be thought worthy who has trampled the Son of God underfoot, counted the blood of the covenant by which he was sanctified a common thing, and insulted the Spirit of grace?"* (Hebrews 10:29 NKJV)

So please forsake your sin when confessing it to God. Many won't confess their sins; they will hide them from people and ignore or silence the voice of God in their conscience. Don't let it get to that state; if it does, you become a candidate for untimely death, that is, dying before your God-appointed time and season. The scripture says,

> *"He who covers his sins will not prosper, But whoever confesses and forsakes them will have mercy"* (Proverbs 28:13 NKJV).

Do not quench your light by covering your sins; confess and forsake them. Many believers are dying because of unconfessed or hidden sin.

4. Draw Close to God

The fourth thing is closeness to God. Make sure you are deeply connected to God. Many things take believers unaware because they are not walking in close fellowship with God. Being born again is just the first step; we must then make a conscious effort to walk in Him, continuing in the light and keeping His commands (cf. 1 John 1:7; 2:3–6; 2:28). Jesus said in John 17:3,

> *"And this eternal life that they may know you the only true God and Jesus Christ whom you have sent."*

So, receiving Jesus Christ is an invitation to know God. Many don't take advantage of this, so they fall short of the glory that God has for them in Christ Jesus. They live like mere men and die like mere men. The scripture says,

> *"Draw near to God, and He will draw near to you."* (James 4:8 NKJV)

This scripture was written to believers, so God is telling you, the believer, to draw near. The scriptures say,

> *"For behold, those far from you shall perish."* (Psalm 73:27 NKJV)

> *"I said, 'You are gods, And all of you are children of the Most High. But you shall die like men, And fall like one of the princes.'"* (Psalm 82:6–7 NKJV)

You don't want to be far from God; you want to be close to Him so He can reveal the secrets of your life that eyes cannot see or ears cannot. Let every day be an opportunity for you to draw near to God.

> *"But as it is written: 'Eye has not seen, nor ear heard, Nor have entered into the heart of man The things which God has prepared for those who love Him.'"* (1 Corinthians 2:9 NKJV)

5. Remain Spiritually Watchful

You must be watchful and not get carried away by worldly pleasures. If you do, the enemy will come to you unawares. Remember
that after David prayed to God that his times were in God's hands,
he followed that prayer with a prayer to God to deliver him from
his enemies (Psalm 31:15–16). You can't pray these kinds of prayers
if you are not watching. Proper watching allows you to know what
to pray and when to pray. Praise the Lord.

6. Engage in Spiritual Warfare

You must engage in warfare using the entire armor of God as stated
in Ephesians 6:10–18, and you must fight as a good soldier and be
on your guard. Fighting the battle that God has called you to fight
guarantees that you are always in alignment with God, which will
make it difficult for the enemy to snatch your life away.

7. Maintain Spiritual Freedom

You must learn how to stay free spiritually and avoid spiritual
bondage. This will mean living a consecrated life devoted to God
and His purposes and avoiding getting entangled with the affairs
of this world. It is through sin and worldly corruption that the
enemy uses to bring people into captivity, and you must prevent
these things, by all means, to stay free.

The Deadly Consequence of Specific Sins

Last but not least, sins that lead to early graves. Some sins will lead
to an untimely death if one continues in them and doesn't repent
from them quickly. For example, the sin of sexual immorality is
one of those sins. The scripture says,

"Do you not know that you are the temple of God and that the Spirit of God dwells in you? If anyone defiles the temple of God, God will destroy him. For the temple of God is holy, which temple you are." (1 Corinthians 3:16–17 NKJV).

The scripture says:

"Flee sexual immorality. Every sin that a man does is outside the body, but he who commits sexual immorality sins against his own body" (1 Corinthians 6:18 NKJV)

Therefore, we know that sexual immorality will lead to the defilement of God's temple, which is your body, and that will attract the judgment of God, which could lead to an untimely death for the believer in Christ Jesus.

How Death Entered the World

Introduction

How did death enter the world? Was death part of God's original plan for humanity? In this chapter, we will explore the origin of death according to Scripture, understand its relationship with sin, discover Christ's victory, and learn the practical implications for our lives today.

The Original Design

When God created Adam and Eve, He gave them commandments by which to live. The scripture says,

> *"Then the Lord God took the man and put him in the garden of Eden to tend and keep it. And the Lord God commanded the man, saying, 'Of every tree of the garden you may freely eat; but of the tree of the knowledge of good and evil you shall not eat, for in the day that you eat of it you shall surely die.'"* (Genesis 2:15–17 NKJV)

God made it clear that disobedience would lead to death. This implies that as long as they obeyed God's command, they would not experience death. Therefore, we conclude that death was not part of God's original intention for humanity. Death came as a consequence of disobedience. God's word is life, and whatever He speaks comes to pass, even if it does not exist when the word is spoken. Death did not exist before Adam's disobedience. The scripture says,

> *"God calls those things which do not exist as though they did"* (Romans 4:17 NKJV).

By this, we understand that death did not exist before the fall of man. When God warned Adam and Eve not to eat the fruit, death did not yet exist; it would not have existed if they had obeyed God's command.

The Fall and Its Consequences

This initial warning in Genesis finds its theological explanation in the New Testament, where Paul writes in Romans 5:12,

> *"Therefore, just as through one man sin entered the world, and death through sin, and thus death spread to all men because all sinned."*

From this scripture, we see that death came through sin. Through Adam's disobedience, death entered the world. The scripture in Romans 5:12 highlights that death resulted from sin. Death did not come in isolation; sin brought death, and without sin, there would be no death. Sin and death are intrinsically linked. Romans 6:23 states,

> *"For the wages of sin is death, but the gift of God is eternal life in Christ Jesus our Lord."*

Sin precedes death, and for death to reign in life, sin must first reign. That is why, to defeat death, God had to first address the issue of sin. For God to remove death, He had to deal with the issue of sin first.

Consider how this plays out in our everyday lives: when we choose to harbor bitterness or unforgiveness, we experience a kind of relational death as our connections with others wither. When we engage in dishonesty, we experience the death of trust. These are tangible manifestations of how sin leads to various forms of death in our lives, even before physical death occurs.

Christ's Victory Over Death

Having established how death entered the world, we can now understand the significance of God's redemptive plan through Christ. This is why, to give us life, God dealt with sin through Jesus Christ, the Lamb of God who takes away the sin of the world (John 1:29). By taking away the world's sins, Jesus gives life to the world (John 6:33).

Jesus Christ conquered death by conquering sin. 1 Corinthians 15:55–56 says,

> "O Death, where is your sting? O Hades, where is your victory? The sting of death is sin, and the strength of sin is the law."

The sting of death is sin, and the strength of sin is the law. This passage shows that the sting of death is sin, and the power of sin is the law. Notice how God addressed the root cause of death through Jesus Christ. God didn't just tackle sin; He addressed it at its root. Since the strength of sin is the law, God introduced a new way by which we can achieve righteousness through Jesus Christ, apart from the law, thereby weakening sin by removing its strength, which is the law. Praise God!

The Operation of Death

Just as death entered the world and affected every life, so too, if sin is at work in you, then death is also at work in you. Just as death entered the world through one man's sin (Rom 5:12), it enters every individual life the moment sin takes hold. That entry is first a matter of spiritual death—separation from God's life—long before it reaches its outward, physical expression. In other words, if sin is actively working in you, spiritual death is already present, even if the body has not yet succumbed to physical death. Adam and Eve illustrate the point: although their bodies continued to breathe after they ate the forbidden fruit, they immediately passed from life to spiritual death (Gen 2:17; 3:7–8) and only later experienced bodily decay "to dust" (Gen 3:19).

You may be strong and healthy today, but if sin is reigning in you, your life is like a ticking time bomb. Any day, at any time, the work of death will be perfected in your life, ultimately leading to physical death. But some may ask: Aren't believers in Christ also subject to death? Yes, but it is a different kind of death.

Death and the Believer

True believers in Jesus Christ who have genuinely given their lives to God and live consecrated lives do not die because of sin but because their corruptible bodies have not yet been redeemed, even though their souls have been redeemed. Unbelievers die because of sin as well as because of the corruptibility of the body.

Additionally, believers in Christ, though they may die physically, continue to live in the Spirit; they do not experience spiritual death. As Jesus said in John 11:25–26,

> "I am the resurrection and the life. He who believes in Me, though he may die, he shall live. And whoever lives and believes in Me shall never die."

There is no spiritual death for those who live and die in Christ. However, those who die without Jesus Christ will face a second death (Revelation 21:8).

To illustrate this distinction more clearly: Physical death for the believer is more like a transition than an ending—similar to how we might move from one room to another in a house. For the unbeliever, however, death represents both the physical end of life and a spiritual separation from God. This is why Scripture refers to a "second death" for those who reject Christ—it is not merely the cessation of physical life but an eternal separation from the source of all life, which is God.

Implications for Believers

This theological understanding of death's origin isn't merely academic—it has profound implications for how we live our daily lives. Understanding the concept of death is not just theological but a crucial tool for living a fulfilling life. If the life of Christ is in you, it will lead you to live a fulfilling life in the eyes of God. However, if sin reigns in you, your life may be cut short, and you will leave this world without fulfilling God's plan for your life. This understanding empowers you to make choices that lead to a life of fulfillment and purpose, enlightened by the knowledge of sin and death.

Conclusion

Having understood how death entered the world and how it operates in many lives, be determined that sin will not reign in your life. By doing so, death will not have its way, and when you do die, it will be because God has called you home, not because of the workings of death in you.

Sources of Untimely Death

Introduction

In this chapter, we will examine sources of untimely death. What causes people to die before fulfilling their God-appointed days on earth? We will discuss six primary causes: sin, disobedience to God's commandments, the activity of enemies, spiritual bondage, lack of watchfulness, and inadequate spiritual warfare. Understanding these sources is essential for those who desire to fulfill their divinely appointed lifespan.

First Cause: Sin As A Source Of Untimely Death

The first and most important source of untimely death is sin. God told Adam and Eve that the day they sinned, they would die. This is a stark warning, a reminder of the grave consequences of sin. If you search the scripture, you will find out that sin is the number one reason why many died and did not fulfill their days. The scripture says that the wages of sin is death (Romans 6:23). Also, we see in Romans 5:12 that death came into the world through sin.

Therefore, to avoid untimely death, you must deal with the issue of sin. You must not let sin reign; this is foundational for anyone who wants to fulfill their earthly days. For example, in Proverbs 7:22–23 the scripture talks about how engaging in adultery can end one's life. Not just adultery; if you want to fulfill your days on earth, you must depart from iniquity. Proverbs 10:2 says,

> "Treasures of wickedness profit nothing, But righteousness delivers from death."

Righteous living, as described in the Bible, involves living a life that is pleasing to God, following His commandments, and treating others with love and respect. This is where you should start if you desire to live fully. Commit to righteous living and doing what is right in God's eyes, not in the eyes of men. This is the foundation of building a life of eternal success. The scripture says that if the foundations are destroyed, what can the righteous do? (Psalm 11:3 NKJV). Let your life be built on the foundation of righteousness, and your life will not be cut short before you fulfill your days. Praise the Lord!

Real-Life Examples of Sin's Consequences

I knew this pastor, an assistant general overseer to a very popular man of God. In many churches, the general overseer is a senior leader who is responsible for overseeing the spiritual and administrative affairs of the church. He was engaging in adultery with multiple women and kept it secret until he was exposed. The women began to confess one by one, and he had no choice but to admit to the sin openly. He was immediately suspended by the general overseer and placed under strict disciplinary action. The general overseer's swift and decisive action in this case is a reflection of the seriousness with which the church views sin. He thought the action of the General Overseer was too severe, so he left the church and started his ministry. The ministry took off since he was a gifted preacher, but he died six months later.

There is another popular gospel minister who has been engaging in an adulterous affair for several years, and he always travels to this new country to engage in extramarital affairs with a woman who lives in another country, different from his and his wife's. The woman got pregnant, but the gospel minister asked her to abort the baby. Can you notice how one sin can lead to another? After the woman refused to abort the baby and was threatened, she decided to come forward and confess. When she admitted it, the gospel minister did not deny the affair but instead apologized to his wife. Not long after this came to the open, he died.

Do not think these two examples and many more that you may or may not be aware of are coincidences. They are not. Paul wrote the Corinthians believers in 1 Corinthians 11:30 that most of them are sick and dying because of sin. Therefore, please pay attention to what is being discussed here.

Do not hide your sins until God exposes them. In the two examples I gave, they waited till they were exposed, which is not true repentance; that is why they died regardless.

The will of God in Christ Jesus is that you should not sin, but if you do sin, don't cover it. Repent immediately and forsake it (1 John 2:1, Proverbs 28:13 NKJV). Do not play with sin.

Second Cause: Disobedience To God's Commandments

The second cause of untimely death is disobedience to the commandments of God. If you desire to fulfill your days on earth, then you must take every word of God seriously; don't despise any in any area of your life. Deuteronomy 8:3 says man shall not live by bread alone but by every word that proceeds out of the mouth of God. Every word of God that you hear can give you life (if you obey) or death (if you despise it). Just as you desire bread, you should want the word of God more because it is your life. Job 23:12 says,

> "I have not departed from the commandment of His lips;
> I have treasured the words of His mouth More than my
> necessary food."

This is a call to obedience, a reminder of the life-giving power of God's word. Treasure His commandments more than your necessary food, and you will live.

Can you see how Job treasured the words of God? No wonder, no matter what the enemy had brought upon him, God did not allow the devil to take his life. He did not die in adversity because he stood on a sure foundation.

Biblical Examples of Disobedience's Consequences

The dangers of disobeying any word of God cannot be overemphasized. You could be a servant of God and still die because you disobeyed one command of the Lord, just like Moses was prevented from reaching the promised land because he transgressed the commandment of God (Numbers 20:11–12 NKJV). All the children of Israel who died in the wilderness died because of disobedience. King Saul died because of disobedience. The scripture says in 1 Chronicles 10:13,

> " So Saul died for his unfaithfulness which he had committed against the LORD because he did not keep the word of the LORD, and also because he consulted a medium for guidance."

God has not changed. For He says,

> "I am the Lord, I do not change" (Malachi 3:6 NKJV).

Therefore, if the life of Saul was cut short because of unrepentant sin and transgression against God and His kingdom taken from him and his children and given to David and his descendant, what makes you think that God will not do the same to every believer in Christ who sins and refuse to forsake their sin? He will because He is a just God and will apply the same standard of judgment to all. Therefore, sin strips believers of their inheritance in Christ as well as potentially cutting short their earthly life.

Many examples abound in the scripture of people whose lives were cut short due to disobedience.

If you are living in disobedience, know that you are still alive today because God wants to have mercy on you. You need to be humble and repent and ask God for mercy and cleansing through the blood of Jesus Christ. The scripture says he who covers his sins shall not prosper, but whoever confesses and forsakes them shall obtain mercy (Proverbs 28:13 NKJV). Obedience is the cure for disobedience. This means that you can overcome the consequences of your past disobedience by obeying God's commandments and living a righteous life. Turn the page and follow the voice of God to return to Him (Zachariah 1:3).

Third Cause: The Activity Of One's Enemies

The third cause of untimely death is the activity of one's enemies. This life is a battle, and those who will do anything significant will have physical and spiritual enemies. The first step toward victory over your enemies is to acknowledge their existence; you are doing yourself a disservice if you don't know the strength of your enemies. The scripture says we are not ignorant of the devices of the enemy (2 Corinthians 2:11). Your ignorance itself is a weapon in the hands of those who seek to end your life.

Many pains people experience in life, including death, are not destined by God, nor are they the acts of God. They are the activities of evil. Once you understand this, you will always be on alert and gain enough understanding to wage war against your enemies. Do not say you have faith in God and keep silent amid an attack from your enemies. You do not have faith in God more than King David. Psalm 25:2, David says,

> "O my God, I trust in You; Let me not be ashamed; Let not my enemies triumph over me."

This is the same David who says in Psalm 31:15, "My times are in your hand." He didn't stop there; despite recognizing that his time is in God's hand, he still prayed to God in various situations for God to deliver him from death. What could have happened if he hadn't prayed? He would have died before his time. This is how many have perished because of the activities of witchcraft and human enemies, because they didn't pray to God when their enemies came for them.

Someone may say, But God never sleeps or slumbers; how come He will allow His children to die because they didn't pray? I understand this question, but prayerlessness is a symptom of a broken relationship with God. Prayer is a spiritual activity, and those who are alive to God will be prompted to pray at different times by the Holy Spirit that lives in them. Just as God never sleeps or slumbers, the spirits of those alive in God never sleep or slumber, so their bodies may be resting in a deep sleep, but their spirits are awake and cannot be attacked spiritually. This is why the scripture referred to sinners as the spiritually dead (Luke 9:60). They are spiritually dead because they are not alive to God.

Therefore, the lack of prayers and lack of confidence of many in God's ability to deliver them stems from a lack of relationship with God. The Bible is filled with examples of people whose lives were cut short by their enemies. I am sure you know many people who have died because they were murdered by people who hate them and want them gone.

Fourth Cause: Spiritual Bondage Or Captivity

The fourth reason why people die an untimely death is spiritual bondage or captivity. Everyone born into this world was born into spiritual captivity; we are all born into the kingdom of darkness. Though we are all born into this bondage, the level of spiritual bondage is different, and many factors can contribute to how severe the bondage is. Factors like ancestral or parental sin, one's sin and one's various indulgences in the world, one's enemies, etc, can bring people into different categories of bondage, and the severity of the bondage might impact the individual's lifespan.

Just like people in jail have different cell locations depending on the severity of their crimes, and those on death row have different death dates. However, in spiritual bondage, all its prisoners are on death row, and the day of death chosen by their captors is arbitrary and can occur anytime, and captives don't know their day of death.

> *"Thus says the Lord God: 'Woe to the women who sew magic charms on their sleeves and make veils for the heads of people of every height to hunt souls! Will you hunt the souls of My people and keep yourselves alive? And will you profane Me among My people for handfuls of barley and for pieces of bread, killing people who should not die, and keeping people alive who should not live, by your lying to My people who listen to lies?" 'Therefore, thus says the Lord God: 'Behold, I am against your magic charms by which you hunt souls there like birds. I will tear them from your arms and let the souls go, the souls you hunt like birds."* (Ezekiel 13:18–20 NKJV)

You can see from this passage in Ezekiel 13 that God is describing how many souls are taken into spiritual captivity and killed before their time. God is saying here that many people are dying who should not die. By these, you know that many deaths on earth are not God's will. Therefore, you must understand how spiritual captivity can lead to untimely death so that you can wage war using the weapons that God has provided for you through Jesus Christ to set yourself free and deliver yourself from untimely death, which many experience because of spiritual captivity.

Fifth Cause: Lack Of Watchfulness

The fifth reason people die untimely is a lack of watchfulness—living a carefree life, insensitive to the things of the Spirit. If you are not watching, even though you may be a believer and have been translated to the kingdom of light from the kingdom of darkness (Acts 26:18, 1 Peter 2:9), you could be taken back into bondage, and you could still die untimely without fulfilling your God appointed days. 1 Peter 5:8 says,

> *"Be sober, be vigilant; because your adversary the devil walks about like a roaring lion, seeking whom he may devour."*

The adversary, the devil, will devour you like a roaring lion if you are not vigilant, says the scripture. The scripture also says in Matthew 26:41 that you should watch and pray so that you do not fall into temptation. Watching and praying are important if you desire not to fall into captivity again. Galatians 5:1 says,

"Stand fast therefore in the liberty by which Christ has made us free, and do not be entangled again with a yoke of bondage."

So, there is a possibility of getting into bondage again. You need to stand, watch, pray, and resist the devil continuously to avoid getting into spiritual captivity again.

Sixth Cause: Lack Of Engagement In Spiritual Warfare

The sixth reason for untimely death is a lack of engagement in spiritual warfare. Every believer is in a battle, whether or not they know it. Imagine a soldier battling and entangling himself with worldly affairs; both himself and the people he protects will become war casualties. Jesus Christ has called you to be a soldier, and the scripture says,

"No one engaged in warfare entangles himself with the affairs of this life, that he may please him who enlisted him as a soldier."

Not only is entangling worldly affairs dangerous for a soldier and those around him, but it will also be dangerous if the soldier is unskilled in using the weapons provided for him or if he neglects using the weapons altogether. That is why the scripture says to put on the whole armor of God so that you may be able to stand against the wiles of the devil (Ephesians 6:10 NKJV). Therefore, actively and skillfully engaging in spiritual warfare safeguards against untimely death.

Conclusion: Understanding the Manifestations of Untimely Death

Having given all these sources of untimely death, many may say, what about sickness, accident, old age, and many other causes of death? Please note that for death to manifest, it will manifest through different means, such as through accident, sickness, suicide, etc. However, these are not the root cause; they are just manifestations of the death sentence that is hanging over a soul as a result of the sources we have been discussing.

Just like when someone is sentenced to death, they can either die through a firing squad, lethal injection, or whatever means the state decided to carry out the death sentence. Similarly, there are many living today who have the sentence of death on them spiritually. When this manifests, it manifests in whatever physical means possible to take the life of that soul. Only Jesus Christ can set the captives free, and only He can deliver those who spiritually have the sentence of death hanging over them (Luke 4:18, Hebrews 2:14). Praise God!

Deaths Caused By Sin And Disobedience

Introduction: The Connection Between Sin and Death

This chapter delves into the profound significance of various deaths in the scripture that directly resulted from sin and disobedience to God's commands. It underscores the responsibility of each individual to understand the implications of sin, as we have learned that death is not a standalone consequence; rather, it derives its power from sin.

Adam and Eve: The First Death

We are going to look at the first death in Adam and Eve. They were created to live forever in the garden of God. Their days were not numbered according to the plan of God. However, they sinned through disobedience, and because of that sin, they became subject to death, and eventually, when it was fully manifested, they died. The scripture says in Genesis 5:5 that Adam lived for nine hundred and thirty years, and he died. This may seem like a long time to live, but in the eyes of God, they were not supposed to die. Therefore, they did not fulfill their days. After the fall of Adam, all descendants of Adam became subject to death, and God now numbered their days. Genesis 3:22 says,

> "Then the Lord God said, 'Behold, the man has become like one of Us, to know good and evil. And now, lest he put out his hand and take also of the tree of life, eat, and live forever."

God decided that man will not live forever in his sinful state until he is redeemed. So God had plans for man's redemption and to restore the eternal life they lost due to the transgression of Adam.

Shortened Lifespans: God's Response to Wickedness

Even though God now numbered men's days, their life span was still pretty long, with some living up to almost a millennium like Metusselah, who lived for nine hundred and sixty-nine years before he died (Genesis 5:27). Men continue to live for long until we see in Genesis chapter six where God considerably shortened the lifespan of humanity because of their sin and wickedness. Genesis 6:3 says,

> "And the Lord said, 'My Spirit shall not strive with man forever, for he is indeed flesh; yet his days shall be one hundred and twenty years."

So, because of the wickedness in the world, God did not allow men to live for long. You noticed that even though men fell, the Spirit of God did not leave men completely. So when God said His Spirit will not strive with man forever, it is because His Spirit is trying to make men do what is right in His eyes, but they were not following the leading of the Spirit of God. Therefore, God said My Spirit should not continue to try to make men do what is right forever; I will shorten their lifespan. Thus, we see how sin has been the main factor determining whether men fulfill their days since the beginning of creation.

Rachel: Death Through Deception and Idolatry

The next example is Rachel, Jacob's wife. The scripture says,

> *"Then they journeyed from Bethel. And when there was but a little distance to go to Ephrath, Rachel labored in childbirth, and she had hard labor. Now it came to pass, when she was in hard labor, that the midwife said to her, "Do not fear; you will have this son also." And so it was, as her soul was departing (for she died), that she called his name Ben-Oni, but his father called him Benjamin. So Rachel died and was buried on the way to Ephrath (Bethlehem)."* (Genesis 35:16–19 NKJV)

If you do not understand the history of Rachel and Jacob, you will think this death is a natural death, and you won't think anything about it. This is precisely how we view most deaths today; we examine how the person died and then base our conclusion on that. We do not have access to behavioral history like in most biblical stories, which enables us to connect the beginning of a life to the end of a life. Rachel 's death sentence was issued when she stole her father's household idol in Genesis 31:19. She stole it and hid it from everyone, including Jacob, her husband. Laban, her father, furiously pursued Jacob, thinking Jacob stole the idol. Genesis 31:32 says,

> *"With whomever you find your gods, do not let him live. In the presence of our brethren, identify what I have of yours and take it with you." For Jacob did not know that Rachel had stolen them."*

Jacob was so sure that the idol was not with him or anyone in his camp, and that was why he made such a bold statement, which ended up costing the life of his beloved wife, Rachel. The scripture says death and life are in the power of the tongue (Proverbs 18:21). Jacob's words unknowingly pronounced a judgment that ultimately aligned with Rachel's fate. And Rachel died not because it was God's will but because she stole her father's idol, which is an abominable thing to do for anyone connected to the house of

Jacob. We can prove the root cause of Rachel's death because we know the history, but there are many people dying today whose deaths are a result of sin or disobedience, but we can't say for sure because we don't have the history to connect the dots.

Onan: Self-Interest and Disobedience

Onan is also a good example of someone who died without fulfilling their days on earth. The scripture says,

> "But Onan knew that the heir would not be his; and it came to pass, when he went into his brother's wife, that he emitted on the ground, lest he should give an heir to his brother. And the thing which he did displeased the Lord; therefore He killed him also." (Genesis 38:9–10 NKJV).

Onan sinned by disobeying the command of his father; he was deceitful to his father in that he pretended to him that he was going to do everything he had asked him to do, and he was also self-centered because he was thinking about his gain but not what could benefit the entire family as a whole. His actions greatly displeased the Lord, and so He ended his life. We can get all these insights into why these biblical characters died because they were recorded for our learning.

The Wilderness Generation: Unbelief and Its Consequences

The children of Israel who died in the wilderness are an example and warning for every believer. Numbers 14:2–4 says,

> "And all the children of Israel complained against Moses and Aaron, and the whole congregation said to them, 'If only we had died in the land of Egypt! Or if only we had died in this wilderness! Why has the Lord brought us to this land to fall by the sword, that our wives and children should become victims? Would it not be better for us to

*return to Egypt?" So they said to one another, "Let us select
a leader and return to Egypt."*

They complained and murmured after God told them to possess the land of Canaan. Despite all the miracles God had done before this point, there was still a lot of disbelief in the power of God among them. This unbelief spreads like cancer throughout the camp, and those infected paid dearly for it with their lives, according to the word of the LORD. Numbers 14:11 says,

*"Then the Lord said to Moses: 'How long will these people
reject Me? And how long will they not believe Me, with all
the signs which I have performed among them?'"*

As a result of this transgression, God swore that as many were infected by this unbelief and rebellion would die in the wilderness. True to God's word, they all died in the wilderness (Numbers 26:64–65). When the census was taken again in Numbers 26, all those men twenty years and older who rebelled in Numbers 14 were now dead according to the word of the Lord. Concerning the children of Israel and their conduct in the wilderness, the scripture says in 1 Corinthians 10:4–5,

*"and all drank the same spiritual drink. For they drank of
that spiritual Rock that followed them, and that Rock was
Christ. But with most of them, God was not well pleased,
for their bodies were scattered in the wilderness."*

So, we have established that all the children of Israel who died in the wilderness died as a result of unbelief. And we know that their unbelief manifests itself in various rebellious lifestyles like fornication, adultery, idolatry, etc. Those who refused to entangle themselves with such unclean lifestyles believed in God's promises and kept themselves pure. Their obedience preserved their lives, and they saw the promised land and died only after fulfilling their days on earth.

Judas Iscariot: The Wages of Betrayal

Judas Iscariot died by suicide. He did not die as a fulfilled man. He allowed greed to enter his heart and consume him. His life was cut short not because God planned it so, but because he allowed himself to be deceived by the deceitfulness of sin, and disobedience cost him his life and his place in the eternal kingdom of God and Christ. And the scripture says in Acts 1:24–25,

> *"Then they prayed, 'Lord, you know everyone's heart. Show us which of these two you have chosen to take over this apostolic ministry, which Judas left to go where he belongs."*

They selected Matthias to take his place. What befell Judas was not God's plan for his life, but his unfortunate end was self-inflicted and also the plan of the kingdom of darkness for his life. May that not be your fate. May the plan of evil not come to pass in your life. Amen.

Conclusion: Living and Dying for God's Glory

The truth is that every man and every woman is born for the glory of God. We are born to show forth the glory of God. Due to Adam's transgression, he fell from glory and passed this fallen state to all humanity. That is why the scripture says in Romans 3:23,

> *"For all have sinned and fall short of the glory of God."*

The sin of Adam and our sin have deprived us of this glory, and that is why Christ Jesus came. And in Christ Jesus, your life and your death must be for the glory of God.

> *"For if we live, we live to the Lord; and if we die, we die to the Lord. Therefore, whether we live or die, we are the Lord's."*(Romans 14:8 NKJV)

God is not glorified when we live in disobedience, and the consequences of our sins come upon us, and we die before fulfilling our days. Therefore, we should not tolerate sin, disobedience, or unbelief in God's word. This is fundamental if we seek to exit this world at the time appointed by God.

Untimely Death
Caused By Enemies

Introduction: Understanding the Threat

In this chapter, we will look at how the activities of one's enemies can lead to untimely death. Anyone who will make an impact in the kingdom of God and this world will attract physical and spiritual enemies. These enemies are relentless and will seek the lives of their victims until they destroy them. The scripture says,

> *"The thief does not come except to steal, and to kill, and to destroy. I have come that they may have life, and that they may have it more abundantly. (John 10:10 NKJV)"*

So the devil will try to cut short your life so that you don't fulfill God's will. Men and women jealous of your success can also try to eliminate your life. Given all these threats to one's life, how do we stay alive till we accomplish what God has sent us into the world to do?

David's Example: The Power of Pure Conscience and Prayer

Let's look at David's life. Saul was king when God selected David and anointed him as the successor of Saul. When Saul sensed that the anointing of God was on David and that David was going to be king, he began plotting to end David's life. He tried everything humanly possible to kill David, but he failed. Also, David tried everything, both spiritual and physical, to make sure Saul did not kill him. Why did Saul not succeed in killing David? He failed because David was physically and spiritually alert and maintained relationships with God through pure conscience and a devoted life of prayer.

The Role of Conscience

David kept a pure conscience towards God. Despite Saul's hatred, David maintained a pure conscience before God and refused to dishonor him. He continued to honor and respect Saul as the anointed of God. 1 Samuel 18:6–7 says:

> "Now it had happened as they were coming home, when David was returning from the slaughter of the Philistine, that the women had come out of all the cities of Israel, singing and dancing, to meet King Saul, with tambourines, with joy, and with musical instruments. So the women sang as they danced and said: 'Saul has slain his thousands, And David his ten thousand.'"

Notice how David did not allow this public praise to enter his head and make him disrespect Saul. He kept pride far away from himself. The scripture says pride goes before destruction and a haughty spirit before a fall (Proverbs 16:18). We can see that David's faith in God would not have been enough to save him from King Saul if he had not had a good conscience. I believe that his good conscience and faith in God kept him from being killed by Saul.

David fought many wars and had enemies who wanted him dead, but he triumphed over them all because he had a strong faith in God and a good conscience. Even when Absalom, his son, overthrew him, slept with his concubines in full view of the public, and was more than willing to end David's life, he still extended mercy to his son. 2 Samuel 18:5 states that David begged Joab, Abishai and Ittai not to kill Absalom and that they should be gentle towards him despite everything he did to David his father. This is why David was a man after God's heart, and throughout his lifetime, not once did any of his enemies triumph over him. So we see that a man's enemies, physical or spiritual, will try to end his life, but whether they will succeed or not depends on the man's faith in God and his conscience. Paul told Timothy in 1 Timothy 1:19 that those who put their conscience away because of faith have made a shipwreck of themselves. There is no question that your faith cannot stand without a pure conscience towards God and men.

Jesus Christ: Protected Until His Appointed Time

The devil also planned to kill Jesus Christ before His appointed time to depart this world. But we see that every time they tried to lay hands on Him to kill Him, they never succeeded until the appointed time when Judas Iscariot betrayed Him into the hands of the Pharisees. In John 8:59, the Pharisees tried to stone Jesus, but He hid Himself and walked through the midst of them unnoticed. Why? It wasn't His time. He has not finished the work God has sent Him to do.

Paul's Divine Protection

Paul escaped death several times, intact. There was a scenario where the Jews stoned him and thought he was dead, but after they left him, he mysteriously stood up as if nothing had happened (Acts 14:19–20). This should instill in you a profound confidence in the power of God to keep you and preserve you until you have finished your tasks. Just as Jesus knew the hour of His death (John 13:1), Peter knew it (2 Peter 1:14), and so did Paul (2 Timothy 4:6–7); you should also know when your departure time has come. You may not know the exact day, but you should see the season. That is God's will. The scripture says,

> "Surely the Lord GOD does nothing, Unless He reveals His secret to His servants the prophets" (Amos 3:7 NKJV).

Gedaliah: A Warning Against Carelessness

For example, there is this touching story of Gedaliah, whose enemies, led by Ishmael, killed. He happened to be a good man; however, nothing in the story establishes that he has a close connection with God. Despite that, God sent multiple warnings that Ishmael was planning to kill him; he didn't take the warning seriously but was careless with his enemies, and that cost him his life (Jeremiah 40:13–14). We can learn a lot from this story. We cannot afford to be careless with our enemies. The Lord God has given us several warnings, which are littered all over scripture, about our adversary, the devil, and how he plans to kill us. We should not be ignorant of his devices, and we should not be careless.

The Balance of Divine Sovereignty and Human Responsibility

While our times are ultimately in God's hands (Psalm 31:15), Scripture teaches us that we must remain vigilant. The examples of David, Jesus, and Paul and the cautionary tale of Gedaliah all demonstrate that God's protection works in conjunction with our spiritual alertness and obedience. God's sovereignty does not negate our responsibility to be watchful against our enemies' schemes.

Conclusion: Surviving the Attacks of Your Enemies

In conclusion, though your times are in the hands of God, your enemies, both physical and spiritual, will try to end your life before you fulfill the days and the plan God has for you.

Make sure they fail, maintain a healthy relationship with God so He can reveal secrets to you, and make sure you have a clean conscience towards God and men.

By combining faith in God with practical spiritual disciplines, you can ensure that your enemies' attempts to cause your untimely death will fail, allowing you to complete the purpose for which God has placed you on earth.

Death Caused By Spiritual Bondage

Introduction

In this chapter, we are going to look at deaths caused by spiritual bondage and look at how we can prevent going into spiritual captivity. Spiritual captivity is real, and many people go in and out of captivity throughout their lifetimes. Unfortunately, many never come out of captivity; they die in captivity and do not experience freedom before they depart this world. I have personally witnessed the struggles of individuals in spiritual bondage, and I hope that this chapter will provide guidance and hope to those who are currently in such a situation.

The Israel-Egypt Captivity as a Spiritual Metaphor

I will use the life of the children of Israel as an example to explain this concept of spiritual captivity. Please remember that everything in the Old Testament is a shadow of things to come. The scripture clearly states that what happened to the children of Israel serves as an example for us so that we do not make the same mistake they did.

The life of the children of Israel in captivity in Egypt depicts the life of humanity. The children of Israel were under bondage by the Egyptians, and they suffered immensely as a result of this bondage. They were slaves to their masters, the Egyptians. This is akin to everyone in the bondage of sin and being controlled by the power of sin, just like the children of Israel were being controlled by their master, the Egyptians. The suffering and the pains of the children of Israel were so great that they cried out to God. Please remember that many suffered sicknesses and various kinds of suffering as a result of this captivity, and they died in that captivity before their salvation from Egypt came from God. Exodus 1:14 says,

> "And they made their lives bitter with hard bondage—in mortar, in brick, and in all manner of service in the field. All their service in which they made them serve was with rigor."

This was the kind of bondage the Egyptians subjected the children of Israel to. Imagine going through this bondage and never experiencing freedom until your day of death. It is unthinkable.

Why God Allowed Israel's Captivity

However, someone may ask why God waited for over four hundred years before sending deliverance to Israel. The answer to this question can be found in Genesis 15:13–16, which says,

> "Then He said to Abram: 'Know certainly that your descendants will be strangers in a land that is not theirs, and will serve them, and they will afflict them four hundred years. And also the nation whom they serve I will judge; afterward they shall come out with great possessions. Now, as for you, you shall go to your fathers in peace; you shall be buried at a good old age. But in the fourth generation, they shall return here, for the iniquity of the Amorites is not yet complete."

There were already people occupying the land God had promised to Abraham and his descendants; the people occupying these lands were already in idolatry and did not know God or serve Him. Therefore, there was a judgment of God that was to come upon them. Still, their sins against God had not reached the point where God would displace them and give the land to the children of Israel. That would have been unfair in the eyes of God, and since God is bound by His character, everything He does is righteous and just.

The scripture says God is just and righteous in all His ways (Psalm 145:17), but most people don't understand this. It is a fundamental characteristic of God that everyone who wants to have a healthy relationship with God should understand. God can do no wrong. The scripture says righteousness and justice are the foundation of His throne (Psalm 89:19). So, God is good. Therefore, we now know the delay is because the Amorite's iniquity was incomplete, and judging the Egyptians took time. We must believe God's word above everything else because God cannot lie. Men may lie, but God cannot, and everything God says about Himself and His kingdom is an eternal truth that is established forever. The scripture says in Isaiah 40:8,

> "The grass withers, the flower fades, but the word of our God stands forever."

Now that we know why it took four hundred years for deliverance, let's move on.

God's Deliverance Through Moses

So the cry of the children of Israel came to God, and He heard their cries and suffering which they suffered from the hands of the Egyptians. He then sent deliverance through the hands of Moses to deliver the children of Israel from captivity. Please pay attention to this because this deliverance the children of Israel experienced through Moses is akin to the deliverance that every man shall experience from sin through Jesus Christ.

The Parallel Between Moses and Jesus

The scripture says,

> "For the law was given through Moses, but grace and
> truth came through Jesus Christ" (John 1:17 NKJV).

Therefore, we can say God sent Moses to deliver the children of Israel from Egypt and gave the law of God that will make them holy before God, but He sent Jesus Christ to deliver every human from sin and gave them grace through Jesus Christ to make them holy before Him. What a great and loving God we have, who will never rest until He gives deliverance to every soul of man that calls unto Him for salvation. The scripture says,

> *"And it shall come to pass that whoever calls on the name*
> *of the Lord shall be saved."(Act 2:21 NKJV)*

If you are a captive of satan through sin today, please know right now that it is not God's will for you to die in that captivity; through His lovingkindness, He has sent deliverance to you in the person of Jesus Christ. Jesus Christ is God's deliverance for you and God's redemptive plan for all humanity.

Signs of Spiritual Bondage

Now that we have established that the bondage of the children of Israel to the Egyptians is akin to the spiritual bondage that many humans experience under the power of sin. What is the result of this spiritual bondage? Untimely death, as well as eternal separation from God, which is eternal death. The scripture says,

> *"The wages of sin is death, but the gift of God is eternal life*
> *through Jesus Christ our Lord"(Romans 6:23 NKJV).*

How do you know you are in bondage to sin? You are in bondage to sin if the power of sin is controlling your conduct. For example, you are sexually immoral, and you can't help it; even if you decide that you don't want to continue that lifestyle, it is not up to you. You find yourself in it again because the power of sin working in you is keeping you in bondage to this sin. In essence, all those under the power of sin, who cannot control their desires and are slaves to sinful desires like:

- fornication
- adultery
- greed
- homosexuality
- Drunkenness
- lust
- and more

are all under the power of sin and are in spiritual bondage.

The Two Kingdoms: Light and Darkness

Please note that the father of sin is the devil. Sin was introduced into the world by Satan; therefore, if you are in spiritual bondage as a result of sin, then you are under the power of darkness and Satan. The scripture says in John 10:10,

> "The thief does not come except to steal, kill, and destroy. I have come that they may have life and that they may have it more abundantly."

Therefore, if you are under the power of Satan, it means he can end your life whenever he so desires. This is why you need to believe in the gospel of Jesus Christ so that you can be translated from Satan's kingdom into the kingdom of God.

In Acts 26:17–18, Jesus told Paul and said:

> "I will deliver you from the Jewish people, as well as from the Gentiles, to whom I now send you, to open their eyes, in order to turn them from darkness to light, and from the power of Satan to God, that they may receive forgiveness

of sins and an inheritance among those who are sanctified by faith in Me."

From this scripture, we know that all those who don't know God and who are living in sinful conduct are under the power of Satan and in the kingdom of darkness.

Every living human is in one of these kingdoms:

1. The kingdom of light

2. The kingdom of darkness

The kingdom of light is the kingdom of God and Christ. Those in the kingdom of God are those whose lives are powered by God through the Holy Spirit. At the same time, those in the kingdom of darkness are those whose lives are being influenced by fleshly desires and demonic spirits.

The kingdom you belong to while you live on earth is your eternal kingdom, where you spend eternity. Notice Acts 26:17–18 states the qualification for entering the kingdom of God. It says those who receive forgiveness of sins; by this, we know that the presence of sin in any life makes them members of the kingdom of darkness and under the power of Satan. That is why people need to receive forgiveness for their sins before being admitted into the kingdom of God.

The Danger of Returning to Captivity

The presence of sin admits you into Satan's kingdom, but the absence of sin grants you access to the kingdom of God. Since sin is what determines which kingdom you belong to, it also implies that if you continue sinning after coming to Jesus Christ, you can become captives of satan and become subject to his authority again, meaning he could decide to end your life any day.

Just like after the children of Israel were delivered from Egypt and because they did not keep the commandments of the Lord, they were taken captive again multiple times by various of their enemies, notably their captivity in Babylon, which came as a result of complete rebellion against the ways of God. Many of them died in that captivity.

The Path to Spiritual Freedom

So when you give your life to Jesus Christ, you must ensure you don't continue sinning. Quickly repent if you fall into sin. The scripture says in Proverbs 28:13, "He who covers his sins will not prosper, but whoever confesses and forsakes them will have mercy." You will not prosper if you cover your sins because your sins will bring you under the power of Satan and his kingdom, and nothing good comes out of the kingdom of darkness. You will get pain and sorrows, and, eventually, your life will be cut short, and you will not fulfill your days on earth.

Also, the scripture says in 1 John 1:9,

> "If we confess our sins, He is faithful and just to forgive us
> our sins and to cleanse us from all unrighteousness."

Therefore, confessing your sins and turning away from them when you fall keeps you in the kingdom of God and ensures that you don't get entangled again by the power of Satan and become subjective again to his government. May the Lord keep you.

Conclusion

In summary, the way to prevent your life from being cut short without fulfilling your God-given days on earth is to repent of your sins, put your faith in Jesus Christ, and learn to walk in the ways of God. If you fall into sin as a believer in Jesus Christ, quickly repent and do not return to that sin again. The power to stay pure in Jesus Christ comes from the Holy Spirit that is given to you the day you repent and put your faith in Jesus Christ. It is my prayer that you will fulfill your days on earth and that no power of satan will cut your life short.

Avoiding Untimely Death Through Spiritual Freedom

In this chapter, I will dive deeper into how to avoid untimely death through spiritual freedom. I have stated that untimely death in this context is dying without fulfilling your days; it is dying outside the will of God. It implies that someone dies at a time not appointed by God but through the will of their oppressor, the devil.

The Foundation: Understanding Spiritual Captivity

In the previous chapter, I tackled how anyone who is in sin and has not repented and placed their faith in Jesus Christ is under the power of satan and in the kingdom of darkness. Anyone in captivity under the control of sin will die according to the will of Satan, not according to God's plan. In captivity, your life and everything about your life is controlled by the will of your captors. Therefore, the first step towards fulfilling your days on earth is to ensure that you are not captive to sin and subject to the dictates of the kingdom of darkness.

So, spiritual freedom is necessary for all those who want to fulfill their days on earth. However, you cannot obtain spiritual freedom or stay free by your will or power. That is why God sent Jesus Christ. Many people mistake the coming of Christ as though He came to save people from some physical oppressor or anything physical. Even the disciples of Jesus Christ asked Him in Acts 1:6–7 if He was going to restore the physical kingdom of Israel. However, Jesus let them know His kingdom is an everlasting kingdom, and primarily, He came to liberate people who are captives of the satanic kingdom and bring them into the kingdom of God.

Christ's Mission of Liberation

"For God so loved the world that He gave His only begotten Son, that whoever believes in Him should not perish but have everlasting life."(John 3:16 NKJV)

Therefore, Jesus Christ came to set you free from the grips of the satanic kingdom and give you eternal life. Announcing His ministry in Luke 4:18, Jesus Christ said:

"The Spirit of the LORD is upon Me, Because He has anointed Me To preach the gospel to the poor; He has sent Me to heal the brokenhearted, To proclaim liberty to the captives And recovery of sight to the blind, To set at liberty those who are oppressed."

Jesus Christ came to deliver those spiritual captives of Satan from every kind of oppression and to set them free to serve the living God.

Therefore, the first step towards spiritual freedom is to be born into the kingdom of God. How do you get born into the kingdom of God? Repentance towards God and faith towards the Lord Jesus Christ (Acts 20:21). True spiritual freedom comes through faith in Jesus Christ. John 8:32 says,

"Therefore if the Son makes you free, you shall be free indeed."

If Jesus Christ, the only begotten Son of God, sets you free, you will be free indeed, and no power of darkness can hold you bound again.

When you put your faith in Jesus Christ, the sin that makes it impossible for you to have fellowship with God will be washed away by the blood of Jesus Christ. Going forward, your life will be under the power of God instead of under the control of Satan, and you will also be translated from the kingdom of darkness into the kingdom of light. In Acts 26:17–18, Jesus Christ spoke to Paul and said,

> *"I will deliver you from the Jewish people, as well as from the Gentiles, to whom I now send you, to open their eyes, in order to turn them from darkness to light, and from the power of Satan to God, that they may receive forgiveness of sins and an inheritance among those who are sanctified by faith in Me."*

The Symptoms of Spiritual Captivity

From this scripture, we see many symptoms of spiritual captivity: spiritual blindness, where you can't discern the acts of God or the acts of the devil; darkness, because the kingdom of Satan is complete and thick darkness and those who dwell in captivity are living in darkness, they are under the power of Satan, imagine being under the power of your archenemy? Secondly, they still have their sins, and the power of darkness is tormenting them because of these sins. Finally, they have no inheritance in God; they have nothing for them in the everlasting kingdom of God and Christ. You wouldn't wish this for your enemy, right?

No one who can see remains in the kingdom of darkness; that is why Satan uses blindness to keep people in his kingdom. If someone dwells in thick darkness, they will never know the state of their garment or the condition of their appearance. Satan and his demons keep people in their kingdom and under their power through spiritual blindness. That is why the first thing that Jesus Christ, your redeemer, will do for you is to open your eyes. That is why the first thing Jesus Christ said He was sending Paul to do for the Gentiles was to open their eyes(Acts 26:18).

Jesus: The Light That Dispels Darkness

Therefore, do not let anyone deceive you; you need Jesus. Jesus Christ is the light that helps you walk away from darkness. In John 12:46, Jesus said,

> "I have come as a light into the world, that whoever believes in Me should not abide in darkness."

Satan can offer you the world to keep you from talking or learning about Jesus Christ. Jesus Christ is the only escape from the grip of Satan and his kingdom. Nothing else can, and nothing else will.

The Urgency of Spiritual Freedom

So, what have I been saying thus far? If you are not in Christ Jesus, then Satan has authority over your life. Isn't that scary enough for you to run and give your life to Jesus Christ? If you are not in Christ, then the power to end your earthly life is still the hands of the devil, and you are just a time bomb waiting to be destroyed. It is not a good state, and that is why those of us who understand the unsaved man's spiritual state preach the gospel with much urgency.

> "Inasmuch then as the children have partaken of flesh and blood, He Himself likewise shared in the same, that through death He might destroy him who had the power of death, that is, the devil, and release those who through fear of death were all their lifetime subject to bondage."(Hebrews 2:14–15 NKJV)

Please note that this freedom from the fear of death or the power of death is only for those who come to God through Jesus Christ. The deliverance obtained is for everyone, but only upon those who believe in the Lordship of Jesus Christ over their life.

Living in Divine Protection

For those who have come to Christ and are living their lives for Him, please know that Satan cannot end their life, and they will depart this world in God's own time. But some may say, don't we see believers dying daily through unfortunate circumstances? Yes, and there could be two explanations for this. They may be a believer in the name only, or believers who were once saved but did not remain in the freedom Christ has purchased for them, but got entangled in sin and continue a lifestyle of unrepentant sin.

Those who continue a lifestyle of unrepentant sin will make themselves captives of Satan's kingdom again. While believers can sin, they are expected to repent and turn away from it. 1 John 1:9 says,

> "If we confess our sins, He is faithful and just to forgive us
> our sins and to cleanse us from all unrighteousness."

This scripture shows how confessing and forsaking your sins cleanses you from all unrighteousness, making it impossible for the enemy to hold you. As long as the devil has nothing in you, the blood of Jesus Christ is continuously cleansing you, and you are not hiding or loving your sins, you will remain free to serve God, and no power of the enemy can harm you.

Therefore, no one can tell their spiritual state at death except for the individual involved. Consequently, we cannot speculate or take it as a norm that Satan can kill or end the life of a disciple of Jesus at will.

Biblical Examples of Divine Protection

Secondly, many disciples of Jesus Christ were killed under the influence of Satan and his demonic spirits. They were influencing men to end the life of these servants of God, and men also ended the earthly life of Jesus Christ. However, you will notice that even though all these disciples died in unfortunate circumstances, none died before accomplishing their God-given task.

No matter how long or how short they lived, if they are disciples of Jesus Christ, no one or no circumstances can take their life if God still has an assignment for them on earth. This is the truth of God's word. There is no way Satan or any situation on earth can take your earthly life away if God still has an agenda for you on earth.

In John 8:58–59, we see that the Pharisees wanted to stone Jesus to death because He declared His divinity. He made them understand that He existed before their father Abraham did; you could see that Jesus divinely and mysteriously escaped from them because it was not His time to die.

Also, we saw in Acts 14:19–20 how some Jews stoned Paul and left him, thinking he was dead. But when the disciples found him, he arose like nothing had happened. This is another instance of divine protection from God for those in His kingdom and under His authority.

When it was time for Jesus Christ to depart this world, and after being arrested and delivered to Pilate to be crucified, Pilate asked Jesus,

> "Do you not know that I have power to crucify You, and power to release You? Jesus answered, saying to him, "You could have no power at all against Me unless it has been given to you from above" (John 19:10–11 NKJV).

Therefore, you can see that even though Jesus was delivered into the hands of those who sought His life, Jesus made it clear that the only reason was because God had allowed it to happen.

Living Without Fear

Doesn't this give you confidence that nothing happens to you without God's approval once you are in the kingdom of God? And if God approves these events, you can rest assured that they will work together for your overall good. The scripture says,

"And we know that all things work together for good to those who love God, to those who are the called according to His purpose" (Romans 8:28 NKJV).

This should give you confidence in God so that you do not fear whatever comes your way. Our God is the most high, and a believer should never be afraid of anything. That is why David said in Psalm 27:1,

"The LORD is my light and my salvation; Whom shall I fear? The LORD is the strength of my life; Of whom shall I be afraid?."

Also, the Psalmist says in Psalm 46:1–3,

"God is our refuge and strength, a very present help in trouble. Therefore we will not fear, even though the earth be removed, and though the mountains be carried into the midst of the sea; Though its waters roar and be troubled, though the mountains shake with its swelling."

These are the reasons why a believer should have complete confidence that there is no way their life will be cut short before God's appointed time. He who keeps you will not sleep or slumber. (Psalm 121:1–3).

Summary

In summary, believers in Jesus Christ are no longer under the power of sin and death, Satan's authority, or his kingdom. Nothing can happen to them without God's approval. Their lives cannot be cut short before they fulfill their days in Christ Jesus. God will make sure they fulfill their days according to His word. This promise we have from God, and so shall it be. Amen!

Living In Obedience

This chapter will explore the profound concept of living completely by obeying God's word. I will explain how this obedience can help you fulfill your days and avoid untimely death. Additionally, I will illuminate the stark contrast between the life of obedience in the Old Testament, which was centered on adherence to Moses' laws, and the life of obedience in the New Testament, where obedience results from our reliance on the grace of Jesus Christ.

Overview: The Path to Godly Obedience

This chapter will help you understand faithful biblical obedience—from its foundation in salvation to its practical application through the Holy Spirit's power. We will explore how obedience protects you from spiritual danger and ensures you fulfill God's divine purpose for your life.

The Prerequisites of Obedience: Salvation in Christ

First of all, let me categorically state that a sinner, that is, the one who has not repented and has not put their faith in Jesus Christ, cannot live a life of obedience to God. They are not in the kingdom of God. They are in the kingdom of darkness and under the power of Satan. The only thing keeping them alive is that Satan and demonic spirits are not done with them yet, or God, by

His sovereign power, has diverted the attention of their enemies away from their lives to give them more time to repent, and this diversion is unknown to their enemies. That is how powerful God is; even the devil does many things according to the will of God, which is unknown to him. For example, the scriptures say in 2 Corinthians 2:8,

> *"which none of the rulers of this age knew; for had they known, they would not have crucified the Lord of glory."*

So, even when Satan was orchestrating the death of Jesus Christ through ungodly men, he did not even know that he was acting by God's will. He was doing God's will, unknown to him; he only succeeded in killing Jesus when it was time for Jesus Christ to depart the world. Before that time, he had tried multiple times to use the scribes and Pharisees to seize Jesus and kill Him, but he failed. (John 7:30, John 8:20, John 10:39). This should give you confidence in the power of God, that once you are in His kingdom and doing His will, no power of the enemy can hurt you or end your life before you fulfill your days on earth(Luke 10:19). Therefore the first steps towards fulfilling your days as stated in earlier chapters, is to repent of your sins and put your faith in Christ Jesus. This will take you from being under the power of Satan to the power of God and from the kingdom of darkness to the kingdom of light. If you love your life, you won't waste time accepting Jesus Christ as your Lord and Savior.

Now that you are in Christ, you need to live a life of obedience to God. This will guarantee that you are constantly under His authority and power and will ensure that you don't get entangled again in bondage and back under satan's power and kingdom.

Old Testament vs. New Testament Obedience

In the Old Testament, living in obedience required following every detail of Moses' laws; however, in the New Testament, living a life of obedience means a total reliance on the grace of Jesus Christ to save and keep you from sin. The Scripture in John 1:17 says,

*"For the law was given through Moses, but grace and truth
came through Jesus Christ."*

This grace and divine empowerment are the key to your salvation and your freedom from sin. The plan and the intent of God
for the people of Israel after their deliverance from slavery is the
same as His plan and purpose for every sinner who comes to God
through Jesus Christ. The plan is that they should live a holy and
consecrated life dedicated to the worship of God and the services
of His kingdom. However, the requirement for achieving this plan
of God is not the same. The children of Israel need to obey every
law of Moses to accomplish this, while believers in Jesus Christ
need to depend on the grace of Jesus Christ to fulfill their call-
ing in Christ. That is why the Scripture says grace and truth came
through Jesus Christ. Why? Because it is through the grace of Jesus
Christ that you will be saved. (Acts 15:11)

Having established this fundamental distinction, we can now
examine how this grace operates.

Living Through Grace: The Practical Path

Now that we know that living in obedience requires total dependence on the grace of the Lord Jesus Christ, what does this look
like? How does this grace keep you free from sin? In the new cove-
nant, you will be saved by grace (Ephesians 2:8). You are delivered
from the power of sin through grace (Romans 6:14). This grace is
not just a concept; it's a reality that sets you free and liberates you
from the chains of sin. At the same time, the Old Testament has
many laws to follow to achieve God's righteousness. In the New
Testament, God's righteousness is fulfilled through Jesus Christ if
we walk after the Spirit of God (Romans 8:1–2). We need to learn
to follow God's Spirit always, which is easy because our spirit is
now alive to God, and the Spirit of God dwells in us. (Romans
8:9, 1 Corinthians 3:16, 1 Corinthians 6:19, 2 Timothy 1:14). The
people of the Old Testament, Israel, do not have the Spirit of God
in them. Hence, they needed to memorize all the laws of God and

remember to do them, which is why they could not achieve the righteousness of God through the law because it was just practically impossible to do due to the weakness of the flesh(Romans 8:1–3). However, in the New Testament, God plans that you should follow His Holy Spirit and be directed by Him always because He lives in you, and the law of God is written in your heart and not in ink and letters like the Old Covenant(Jeremiah 31:33, Hebrews 8:10, 2 Corinthians 3:3).

The requirement for living an obedient life in Christ Jesus is simple: as you have been set free from the power of sin and the bondage of sin, now use that freedom and yield yourself to the leading of the Holy Spirit; by doing so, you will fulfill the will of God for your life and your days on earth. This simplicity, this straightforward path, should give you confidence and reassurance. You will not die due to the activities of your enemies or satan and his demons. You will depart this world in God's own time.

This divine empowerment through the Holy Spirit provides the foundation for our practical obedience but requires our active participation.

Romans 6:4 says,

> "Therefore we were buried with Him through baptism into death, that just as Christ was raised from the dead by the glory of the Father, even so we also should walk in newness of life."

This is God's will for you; this is how you stay out of bondage. You are free, but don't misuse your freedom. Do not give in to the former lusts to walk according to your former sinful nature. 1 Peter 1:14 says,

> "As obedient children, do not conform yourselves to the former lusts, as in your ignorance."

So, the life of obedience requires you not to conform to your former lusts. Remember, living in disobedience may land you back in Satan's kingdom and under his power if you do not repent and turn away from the life of disobedience against God's command. Galatians 5:13 says,

"For you, brethren, have been called to liberty; only do not use liberty as an opportunity for the flesh, but through love serve one another."

We should not use our liberty to serve the flesh, another term that describes the former lusts. Why? If you serve the flesh, you bring yourself into bondage again. Furthermore, the Scripture says in Galatians 5:16,

"I say then: Walk in the Spirit, and you shall not fulfill the lust of the flesh."

The only way to overcome fulfilling the lusts of the flesh is by walking in the Spirit. That is why the Scripture says in Romans 8:14,

"For as many as are led by the Spirit of God, these are sons of God."

Those who can achieve sonship in the new birth of Jesus Christ walk according to the Spirit of God.

This understanding of walking in the Spirit naturally leads us to consider a common question about grace and obedience.

Now, someone may say, didn't Christ Jesus pay all the price, and why must I walk by the Spirit to remain free? The grace that Jesus gives and will give if you ask is the ability to do the will of God. Scripture says in John 1:12,

"But as many as received Him, to them He gave the right to become children of God, to those who believe in His name."

So, through believing in Jesus Christ and His sacrifice for you, you are set free from sin and given the power to live the life of God. What you do with this power determines whether you stay free or not. Paul admonished the Corinthians believers in 2 Corinthians 6:1:

"We then, as workers together with Him, also plead with you not to receive the grace of God in vain."

He is pleading with them not to receive God's grace in vain. This implies that many Christians will receive the grace and empowerment that comes from above and will still do nothing about it. These are the kind of believers whose lives do not reflect the character of God despite their public profession of faith in Jesus Christ. They have received the grace of God in vain; they did nothing with it. They return to their former lusts and continue to live their lives like other sinners who do not know God. As a believer, you must understand God's will and lean on His grace to accomplish it. The way back to spiritual captivity and back under the power of Satan is rebellion and living life in opposition to the will of God.

Spiritual Warfare: Resisting the Enemy

The will of God for believers in Jesus Christ that will keep them spiritually free from the power of darkness is a life that is not lived to satisfy the lusts of men. If you don't remember anything I am saying, just remember that God does not want you to follow the lusts of men but to live your life pursuing the will of God. Pursuing the will of God will always bring you into conflict with the lusts of men. Apostle Peter warns believers in 1 Peter 2:11, which says,

> "Beloved, I beg you as sojourners and pilgrims, abstain from fleshly lusts which war against the soul."

Fleshly lusts, also known as the lusts of men, are warring against your soul. To save your soul and, by extension, deliver yourself from the power of Satan and darkness, you need to defeat fleshly lusts. This is the battle God has called you to fight in Christ. The adversary, Satan, will contend with you so that he might try to bring you back into his kingdom. Therefore, you need to resist him. How? By resisting fleshly lusts, as Peter warned us in 1 Peter 2:11, the Scripture says in 1 Peter 5:8-9,

> "Be sober, be vigilant; because your adversary the devil walks about like a roaring lion, seeking whom he may devour. Resist him, steadfast in the faith, knowing that the same sufferings are experienced by your brotherhood in the world."

To live a victorious life in Christ Jesus, you must resist the devil steadfastly (James 4:8).

This resistance to the enemy is manifested through a life of consecration, which brings us to the practical application of obedience.

The natural way to resist the devil is to live a consecrated life dedicated to fulfilling the will of God. 1 Peter 4:1 says,

> *"Therefore, since Christ suffered for us in the flesh, arm yourselves also with the same mind, for he who has suffered in the flesh has ceased from sin, that he no longer should live the rest of his time in the flesh for the lusts of men, but for the will of God."*

This is how you stay free in Christ beyond the devil's power. Staying free in Christ guarantees that your life cannot be cut short before you fulfill your days. It guarantees that you accomplished the plan of God for your life on earth before anything can terminate your earthly life. It gives God complete control over your life and well-being because you are now in His kingdom and under His authority. Do not return to your old sinful life as that will be destructive to you and very disappointing to God, who paid a considerable price through the precious blood of Jesus Christ to deliver you from your old sinful life. The way to honor God for what He has done for you is to live a life that is pleasing to Him. Romans 12:1–2 says,

> *"I beseech you therefore, brethren, by the mercies of God, that you present your bodies a living sacrifice, holy, acceptable to God, which is your reasonable service. And do not be conformed to this world, but be transformed by renewing your mind so that you may prove what God's good and acceptable and perfect will is."*

Nothing you can give God that is acceptable to Him other than living a holy and consecrated life. Jesus gave His body for your life; God required that you also sacrifice your body to preserve what Jesus did for you. Psalm 40:6–8 says,

> *"Sacrifice and offering You did not desire; My ears You have opened—burnt offering and sin offering You did not*

require. Then I said, 'Behold, I come; In the volume of the book it is written of me. I delight to do Your will, O my God, And Your law is within my heart.'"

This Scripture shows that God wants you to do His will above anything else. And His will in Christ Jesus is for you to present your body as a living sacrifice to God. What does it mean for it to be a living sacrifice? It means you are living for God's desire, not yours. Your body has become a means by which God expresses Himself on earth, not your expression. Again, this is how you stay free and liberated in Christ Jesus. If you do this, God will protect your life and keep you till He accomplishes all His plans through your body. Your body will not die because it is now in God's hands and an instrument of righteousness in the hands of God. Romans 6:13 says,

"And do not present your members as instruments of unrighteousness to sin, but present yourselves to God as being alive from the dead, and your members as instruments of righteousness to God."

Divine Protection Through Obedience

Having explored the practical path of obedience, we can now understand the profound protection it offers believers.

If you are not presenting your body as an instrument of righteousness, then you are of no use to God but the devil. We know the devil's end game for any lives he uses and those under his authority. The Scripture says in John 10:10,

"The thief does not come except to steal, kill, and destroy. I have come that they may have life and have it more abundantly."

The devil will mess up your life on earth and will kill you before you get the opportunity to repent and return to God. His endgame is to kill and destroy you in the lake of fire. Now, compare this to God's endgame for your life. Jeremiah 29:11 says,

"For I know the thoughts that I think toward you, says the Lord, thoughts of peace and not of evil, to give you a future and a hope."

God has great plans for your life that will last for eternity. Do not let the devil or the flesh rob you of God's plan for your life. The Scripture says in 1 Corinthians 2:9,

"But as it is written: 'Eye has not seen, nor ear heard, nor have entered into the heart of man the things which God has prepared for those who love Him.'"

God is preparing great things for you; to partake in it, you need to remain in His kingdom and under His authority. Remaining in God's kingdom and being under His authority preserves your life on earth and ensures you inherit all the great blessings God has prepared for you in Christ Jesus.

With this understanding of divine protection, we must remain vigilant against the enemy's constant attempts to draw us away from obedience.

Watch out for the deception of the devil, and he will try to lure you back to the deeds of the flesh so he can take you into captivity again. That is the reason the Scripture says we should be vigilant. Also, the Scripture says we should not be ignorant of satan's devices (2 Corinthians 2:11). His devices have not changed: deception, manipulation, and trying to make you doubt God's word and lose sight of the promise of God for temporal pleasure. Remember how he tempted Jesus Christ to bow to him in exchange for all the glory of the world? (Matthew 4:8–10). Jesus doesn't need the glory of the world, but Satan tempted Him with it anyway. There is a glory that was set before Jesus Christ. The Scripture in Hebrews 12:2 says,

"Looking unto Jesus, the author and finisher of our faith, who for the joy that was set before Him endured the cross, despising the shame, and has sat down at the right hand of the throne of God."

Jesus knew the joy set before Him so He wouldn't fall for the devil's lies or deception. And we know that whatever glory Jesus has in the presence of God, the same glory has been destined for everyone who believed in Him and held on to their faith till the very end. Romans 8:17 says,

> "And if children, then heirs—heirs of God and joint heirs with Christ, if indeed we suffer with Him, that we may also be glorified together."

The glory that awaits Jesus Christ is the same glory that awaits every believer in Jesus. But we must be steadfast in the faith as He was before we become partakers of His glory. The Scripture in Hebrews 3:14 says,

> "For we have become partakers of Christ if we hold the beginning of our confidence steadfast to the end."

Therefore, keep your eyes fixed on Jesus Christ. Do not let any activities of the devil take your eyes off Jesus and the promise that awaits you in the presence of God. Be steadfast in your faith and stay free in Jesus Christ. Amen

Conclusion: The Eternal Perspective of Obedience

As we have seen throughout this chapter, living in obedience to God through the power of His grace is not merely about following rules—it is about remaining in His kingdom, under His protection, and fulfilling His divine purpose for your life. This obedience protects you from premature death, ensures spiritual freedom, and guarantees participation in God's eternal glory.

By understanding the contrast between Old and New Testament obedience, embracing the Holy Spirit's guidance, actively resisting the enemy, and presenting yourself as a living sacrifice, you can experience the fullness of God's promise both in this life and in eternity. The path of obedience is the path to abundant life—now and forever.

Spiritual Warfare

Introduction

In this chapter, I will discuss how you can fulfill your days on earth by engaging in spiritual warfare. There is an ongoing battle between the kingdom of darkness and the kingdom of light, whether you know it or not. The moment you give your life to Jesus Christ, you have now become a member of God's kingdom, which puts you in an active engagement against the satanic kingdom. You must be aware of this and actively engage in this battle because ignorance or lack of engagement might lead to devastating consequences, including untimely death. But fear not, for with spiritual readiness, you can face this battle with confidence and strength.

Understanding Your Enlistment as a Soldier

The scripture says in 2 Timothy 2:4,

> "No one engaged in warfare entangles himself with the affairs of this life, that he may please him who enlisted him as a soldier."

The day you repent, forsake your sins, and give your life to Jesus Christ, you enlist in His army. You are now a soldier of Jesus Christ, and you have a role assigned to you in Christ before the foundation of the world. It is now time for you to discover that role in Christ and do them. 2 Timothy 1:9 says,

> "Who has saved us and called us with a holy calling, not according to our works, but according to His purpose and grace which was given to us in Christ Jesus before time began."

So God has given you a role in Christ Jesus before time began. In addition to your specific duties in Christ Jesus, you must engage in spiritual warfare against the kingdom of darkness actively.

The Nature of Spiritual Battle

Please note that the battle God has called you to fight is not against flesh and blood. The scripture says in Ephesians 6:12,

> "For we do not wrestle against flesh and blood, but against principalities, against powers, against the rulers of the darkness of this age, against spiritual hosts of wickedness in the heavenly places."

You must understand this so that you don't make enemies out of humans, the same people Jesus Christ died for. Instead, your battle will be against the principalities and powers that are waging war against you and the kingdom of God, and most often, they could use human agents to accomplish their mission on earth.

Our Dependence on God's Power

In this battle, you will not rely on your strength; if you do that, you will lose. You do not have what it takes to go against the kingdom of darkness when they come against you. The scripture says in Zechariah 4:6,

> "'Not by might nor by power, but by My Spirit,' says the Lord of hosts."

Therefore, it is not by your power but by the Spirit of God that you will overcome every power of the wicked. The scripture says in Psalm 44:5,

> *"Through You, we will push down our enemies; through Your name, we will trample those who rise up against us."*

Since we rely on God's power to give us victory, we need to leverage the weapons God has provided us to fight this battle. The scripture says in 2 Corinthians 10:3-4,

> *"For though we walk in the flesh, we do not war according to the flesh. For the weapons of our warfare are not carnal but mighty in God for pulling down strongholds."*

The weapons we use to fight and defeat all the enemy's powers are not carnal; they are not weapons we can see with our eyes.

The Armor of God: Your Spiritual Weapons

These weapons are described in Ephesians 6:13-18:

> *"Therefore take up the whole armor of God, that you may be able to withstand in the evil day, and having done all, to stand. Stand therefore, having girded your waist with truth, having put on the breastplate of righteousness, and having shod your feet with the preparation of the gospel of peace; above all, taking the shield of faith with which you will be able to quench all the fiery darts of the wicked one. And take the helmet of salvation, and the sword of the Spirit, which is the word of God; praying always with all prayer and supplication in the Spirit, being watchful to this end with all perseverance and supplication for all the saints."*

1. The Belt of Truth

You must ensure that God's truth guides your life; do not let the truths of God's word get corrupted in your heart. That is how the devil defeats many believers today by making them believe something that the Bible did not say. The word of God is perverted in them, and they are now walking in a lie. Such a believer cannot have victory over the kingdom of darkness. Such a one will be a captive of satan in no time. That is why you must guide God's word in your hearts with all diligence. Do not let anything in the world corrupt it. Proverbs 4:20–22 says,

> "My son, give attention to my words; incline your ear to my sayings. Do not let them depart from your eyes; keep them in the midst of your heart; for they are life to those who find them, and health to all their flesh."

The scripture says the word of God is life and health to those who find it. Because it is your life and health, you must guide and keep it with all diligence. If you lose it or it gets corrupted, you will not find life or health.

2. The Breastplate of Righteousness

The second weapon listed is the breastplate of righteousness. This will provide a defense against any attack from the kingdom of darkness. If you are not living right and allowing sin and unconfessed sin to remain in your life, it means that when the kingdom of darkness attacks you, it will most likely succeed against you and get its wish concerning your life. Sin is what gives demonic entities access to your life. Sin is an open door, and it exposes you to demonic attack. Jesus Christ says in John 14:30,

> "I will no longer talk much with you, for the ruler of this world is coming, and he has nothing in Me."

Even Satan came to Jesus Christ to see if there was something in him that would grant him access to Jesus..

The devil will come for you. Do not be ignorant of this. The scripture says in 1 Peter 5:8,

> "Be sober, be vigilant; because your adversary the devil walks about like a roaring lion, seeking whom he may devour."

Satan will come, and demons will come for your life. Once you are in conflict as a soldier, you must stay alert for your own life and that of others around you. You must not fail the Lord Jesus, who has enlisted you into His army. Your loss is His loss, and your gain is Jesus's gain. Therefore, you must wear this armor of righteousness and walk in righteousness, protecting you from the devil. A sign that God is with you is that you are walking in the light. Walking in light is the same as walking in righteousness. The scripture says in 1 John 1:6,

> "If we say that we have fellowship with Him, and walk in darkness, we lie and do not practice the truth."

Having fellowship with God demands living in righteousness and doing what is right in His eyes; no hidden sin can remain in your life. That is how you will ensure continuous protection from God, and no power of the wicked can come near you. Because the Lord God will be your protector and your shield. Living a holy and consecrated life to God is a spiritual weapon, the breastplate of righteousness that protects you from attacks.

3. Feet Prepared with the Gospel of Peace

The third weapon is the preparation of the gospel of peace, meaning you are witnessing for Jesus Christ. You are sharing the good news with others. You are not keeping to yourself what God has done for you through Christ. This is a powerful weapon in the realm of the spirit, and as the scripture says, it is your sandals; it is what covers your feet. Imagine fighting a war barefoot. Therefore, do not underestimate the power of sharing the gospel with others. Be prepared to share the good news of God in Jesus Christ in and out of season. 1 Peter 3:15 says,

> "But sanctify the Lord God in your hearts, and always be ready to give a defense to everyone who asks you a reason for the hope that is in you, with meekness and fear."

As this scripture says, we should be ready always to tell anyone about the hope in us.

4. The Shield of Faith

The fourth weapon listed is faith—this is the lifeline of your Christian life. You must protect your faith in God. How? Absolute belief in the word of God and His promises. Do not let life situations and circumstances make you begin to doubt the word of God. The devil will use different situations in life to shake your faith so that he might break it. Do not allow him to succeed in weakening your faith in God. The scripture says,

"The just shall live by faith" (Romans 1:17 NKJV).

Your life as a just person is sustained by faith. That is how you please God.

Hebrews 11:6 says,

"Without faith, it is impossible to please God."

Make the word of God your ultimate source of truth, not dreams, not situations, not your experience or other people's experience. All those things will change, but only the word of God will stand forever. Therefore, hold onto it. Let God be true and every person a liar.

5. The Helmet of Salvation

Another weapon we must pay attention to is the helmet of salvation. The helmet of salvation protects your head and your thought life. Do not allow the enemy to feed you thoughts contrary to the hope in Jesus Christ. 1 Thessalonians 5:8 says,

"But let us who are of the day be sober, putting on the breastplate of faith and love, and as a helmet the hope of salvation."

The hope of the Lord Jesus' glory is a powerful weapon against demonic forces. Let that hope keep you. Let the joy set before you in Christ's kingdom keep you. As Paul the Apostle said, Christ in me the hope of glory (Colossians 1:27).

6. The Sword of the Spirit

Another weapon for your spiritual warfare is the sword of the Spirit, the word of God. This is your only offensive weapon. You use it to attack your enemies and destroy them. Make sure you study and meditate on God's word so that when you need it, the Holy Spirit can bring it to your remembrance and give it life. As you speak it over your situation or enemies, they will crumble and be defeated.

7. Prayer in the Spirit

The final weapon is the weapon of prayer. You cannot afford not to pray as a soldier of Jesus Christ. There is a saying that says a prayerless Christian is a powerless Christian. If you don't pray, you make yourself susceptible to demonic attack. Therefore, pray without ceasing (1 Thessalonians 5:17), praying in the Spirit. Seek the baptism of the Holy Spirit with evidence of speaking in tongues if you don't have it already, as that will catapult your prayer life to the new level.

Conclusion

As we have seen throughout this chapter, spiritual warfare is a reality for every believer. Your enlistment as a soldier in Christ's army comes with responsibility and divine empowerment. By understanding the nature of this battle, recognizing your dependence on God's power rather than your strength, and properly utilizing God's seven weapons of spiritual armor, you can stand firm against the kingdom of darkness. Remember that your victory is assured not through your might, but through the Spirit of the Lord of hosts.

Sins that lead to an early grave for the Christian

Introduction

I want to discuss sins that lead to an early grave for a believer. A believer in Christ is different from an everyday sinner. While God may not judge a sinner and allow them to repent, that is not true for the believer. The sinner is under a satanic kingdom; God may not judge them while they live, but Satan may end their life at will. However, for a believer, certain sins may lead to your life being cut short on earth if you engage in them and do not quickly repent and forsake them.

> "If anyone sees his brother sinning a sin that does not lead to death, he will ask, and He will give him life for those who sin that does not. There is sin leading to death. I do not say that he should pray about that." (1 John 5:16 NKJV).

This scripture made us understand that there is a sin unto death.

Sexual Sin and Its Consequences

A Christian who engages in the sin of sexual immorality, like fornication, adultery, homosexuality, and any sexual perversion and does not repent and forsake it but continues in it either intermittently or habitually will likely die as a result of that sin. The day they die, they will die before their God-appointed time, and they will perish and will not inherit the kingdom of God.

Biblical Examples of Judgment on Sexual Sin

Remember how all the children of Israel who engaged in fornication and adultery died in the wilderness because of such sins? That is how many Christians are dying and will die because of unrepentant sexual sins. Their death may seem natural, but they are eaten up by their sins and consumed by them.

When David, the man of God, committed adultery and murder, God said he was going to die for that sin. And God meant it. Why do you think God said he was going to die? Was he the only one committing such acts on the Earth? Why are other people from other nations not dying soon after an adulterous affair or murder? That is because God judges His people continuously, not outsiders. Therefore, do not think that as a child of God, you can freely live in adultery or fornication and expect nothing to happen to you.

> *"So David said to Nathan, 'I have sinned against the Lord.' And Nathan said to David, 'The Lord also has put away your sin; you shall not die. However, because by this deed you have given great occasion to the enemies of the Lord to blaspheme, the child also who is born to you shall surely die.'"* (2 Samuel 12:13–14 14 NKJV)

The Importance of Repentance

David could have died if he hadn't repented of that sin of adultery and murder. David repented after the warning of Nathan the prophet; if he hadn't repented, he would have died. He repented and did not return to the same sin again. Did you see any other place where it was recorded that he committed the same sin again? That is how true repentance works.

Also, just like God sent Nathan to David to remind him of his sins, God will send you a warning if you unfortunately find yourself in sexual sins. He is faithful in giving you time to repent and forsake your sin. David seized the opportunity God gave him and repented of his sins, and that saved his life. Unfortunately, many today take God's warning for granted and continue in their sin until they die unexpectedly or until they are infected with a deadly illness that eats them up until they die. The scripture says in Proverbs 28:13,

> "He who covers his sins will not prosper, but whoever confesses and forsakes them will have mercy."

Confess your sins and forsake them. That is how you avoid the untimely death that comes as a result of unconfessed sin.

God's Higher Standard for Believers

Think of all the children of God in the wilderness who received instant judgment for their sins. God held His people to a higher standard. There is a common misconception that God has stopped judging His people because we are in the dispensation of grace. That is not true. The scripture says,

> "For the time has come for judgment to begin at the house of God; and if it begins with us first, what will be the end of those who do not obey the gospel of God?" (1 Peter 4:17 NKJV)

> *"Therefore, we must give the more earnest heed to the things we have heard, lest we drift away. For if the word spoken through angels proved steadfast, every transgression and disobedience received a just reward."* (Hebrews 2:1–2 NKJV)

Therefore, let us heed and ensure we keep our bodies holy unto God and not engage in things that defile them. If you are in any sexual sin right now, you need to repent immediately before the judgment of God comes upon you. When judgment comes, there will be no more door to repentance. Repent now and keep God's holy house, which is your body.

The Danger of Idolatry

Another destructive sin that can end the life of a Christian if not dealt with is idolatry. Deuteronomy 6:14–15 says,

> *"You shall not go after other gods, the gods of the peoples who are all around you, for the Lord your God is a jealous God among you, lest the anger of the Lord your God be aroused against you and destroy you from the face of the earth."*

In this scripture, you can see God warning the children of Israel that they will die if they go after other gods. This goes beyond just worshipping an established idol. It is giving your heart to anything in the same manner that people who don't know God do, whether they give their hearts to idols, to sexual immorality, or to sexual pleasures. If your hearts prioritize satisfying these ungodly desires above honoring God, that is idolatry, and as promised, God did destroy every one of them that engaged in such acts. We know that we as Christians are held to a higher standard, and if God did not spare them, He would not spare us.

Understanding True Idolatry

Idolatry is giving anything, anyone, the place in our hearts that should only be given to God. It could be full-blown idol worship like witchcraft and various pagan worship. Or it is offering anything the adoration, reverence, or longing that should be for God alone. Exodus 20:3–5 says,

> "You shall have no other gods before Me. You shall not make a carved image for yourself—any likeness of anything in heaven above, in the earth beneath, or the water under the earth; you shall not bow down to them or serve them. For I, the Lord your God, am a jealous God, visiting the iniquity of the fathers upon the children to the third and fourth generations of those who hate Me."

God is a jealous God, and He won't tolerate you giving anything or anyone the glory that belongs to Him. All glory, all honor, and all adoration should go to God and Him alone. Be watchful that you do not deprive God of the glory due to His name. You must fear Him above all else. To fear anything else more than you fear God is idolatry. If you honor anything else more than God, it is idolatry. To give anything else more time than you give to God and the things of God is idolatry. To occupy your heart and mind with anything else more than it is occupied with God and the things of God is idolatry. God said in Isaiah 42:8,

> "I am the Lord, that is My name; and My glory I will not give to another, nor My praise to carved images."

Biblical Examples of Judgment on Idolatry

Many people in the Old Testament died because of idolatry and for violating the law of God. Rachel died from stealing her father's household idol and hiding it (Genesis 31:19); she died during childbirth. It was a death that seemed natural, but underneath were the consequences of stealing an idol. (Genesis 35:16–19).

Many of the Israelites who died in the wilderness died because of idolatry. They allowed themselves to be seduced by the people of the nations around them to leave the Lord God. (Numbers 25:1-3,9). Many Israelites also died in the land of their promise due to idolatry. God hates idolatry. Therefore, be alert, and may God give you discernment so you can recognize what is of God and what is not.

Conclusion

The Bible clearly shows that God holds believers to a higher standard than non-believers. For Christians, certain sins—particularly sexual immorality and idolatry—can lead to an early death if not addressed through genuine repentance. Scripture shows examples of God's judgment falling on His people who committed these sins.

As believers, we must understand that the dispensation of grace does not eliminate God's judgment on His household. Instead, scripture confirms that "judgment begins at the house of God" (1 Peter 4:17). When we engage in sexual sin or give anything else the place in our hearts that belongs to God alone, we risk severe consequences, including premature death.

The good news is that God is faithful in warning us before judgment falls. Like Nathan was sent to David, God will provide opportunities for us to repent. True repentance—confessing and completely forsaking the sin—brings mercy and restoration. But ignoring these warnings can lead to devastating consequences.

Let us, therefore, guard our hearts diligently, keeping our bodies as holy temples for God's presence. May we be quick to recognize and turn from any sin that would separate us from God's purpose for our lives. May we always walk in reverent fear of the Lord, giving Him alone the glory, honor, and devotion He deserves.

Stand in the Liberty Of Christ

Introduction

In this chapter, I will discuss how you can fulfill your days and avoid dying before your God-appointed time by staying in the liberty where Christ Jesus has freed you. This knowledge is essential and crucial, and will help you glorify God and live a fulfilling life on earth.

The Freedom Christ Offers

In Luke 4:18, Jesus says,

> *"The Spirit of the LORD is upon Me Because He has anointed Me To preach the gospel to the poor; He has sent Me to heal the brokenhearted, To proclaim liberty to the captives And recovery of sight to the blind, To set at liberty those who are oppressed."*

In this scripture, we know that Jesus Christ came to set people free from captivity. Those who are in captivity are under satanic power and the kingdom of darkness. We know the kingdom of darkness is responsible for all untimely deaths on earth because all men are under their power except those saved by Jesus Christ.

Understanding Satan's Power of Death

Hebrews 2:14–15 tells us,

> *"Inasmuch then as the children have partaken of flesh and blood, He Himself likewise shared in the same, that through death He might destroy him who had the power of death, that is, the devil, and release those who through fear of death were all their lifetime subject to bondage."*

The reality of this scripture is that Satan has the power of death over every unsaved person. One of Jesus' missions is to release those who are under the bondage of Satan. This freedom from Satan is given only to those who come to God through Jesus Christ; the victory that Jesus accomplished over the devil belongs to them. This is important to understand because even though Jesus delivered everyone from the power of Satan, only those who came to Him received this deliverance.

Now, you know that you are free from the power of death. You are free from the power of the devil. The devil and his demons cannot do with your life as they please anymore. You are no longer under their control. They cannot end your life even if they wish to. They can perform these evils in the lives of those not in Christ Jesus. However, those in Christ Jesus have been set free; hallelujah!

Our Responsibility to Maintain Freedom

You need to ensure that you stay free in Christ. It is your responsibility to keep your freedom, just as it is to turn away from sin and accept Jesus Christ into your life. Guard your salvation with everything you have. Do not lose your freedom for the fleeting pleasures of life. Stay free in Christ and fulfill your days on earth through the power of God, which works mightily in all those in Christ Jesus.

Therefore, the only way to ensure that the powers of darkness do not have control over your life is to stay free in Jesus Christ. There is a possibility of being entangled again in the bondage of demonic power through sin. As Paul warns in Galatians 5:1,

*"Stand fast in the liberty by which Christ has made us free,
and do not be entangled again with a yoke of bondage."*

There is a yoke of bondage, the same yoke that was taken away from you after you repented and gave your life to Jesus Christ. The enemies of your soul will seek to bring you back under that yoke of bondage through the deceitfulness of sin.

Practical Steps to Stand in Liberty

How do you stay free in Christ? The most straightforward answer is to live a consecrated life unto God that produces fruits of righteousness. Avoid sinful conduct, flee worldly lusts, and pursue righteousness. In his letter to Timothy, Paul advises:

"Flee the evil desires of youth and pursue righteousness,
faith, love, and peace, along with those who call on the
Lord out of a pure heart" (2 Timothy 2:22 NKJV).

When you pursue these godly attributes, you will be filled with them. The scripture promises,

"Blessed are they which do hunger and thirst after righteousness: for they shall be filled" (Matthew 5:6).

To keep yourself from the devil's attack and all the powers of the enemies, you need to keep yourself under God's protection. You need to walk in the light to keep yourself under God's protection. 1 John 1:5–6 says,

*"This then is the message which we have heard of him, and
declare unto you, that God is light, and in him is no darkness at all. If we say that we have fellowship with him and
walk in darkness, we lie and do not tell the truth."*

According to this scripture, there is no way we can claim we are having fellowship with God while continuing to walk in darkness and living in sin.

Conclusion

I hope the messages in this book have blessed your heart and given you the light to live the life that God has called you to live and equipped you with the knowledge of God necessary for you to avoid untimely death and fulfill your days. God has a perfect plan for you, and He desires that you fulfill your days on earth above all things. God wants you to maximize the grace of the Lord Jesus Christ so that you live the victorious life that Christ purchased for you. He wants you to get your freedom in Christ and to remain free in Christ. I pray with all my heart that you fulfill your days on earth. Amen.

www.ingramcontent.com/pod-product-compliance
Lightning Source LLC
Chambersburg PA
CBHW052157090426
42741CB00010B/2310